Composite Presence

Composite Presence

Curator
Bovenbouw Architectuur

Contents

6   Memory as a Design Studio   *Sofie De Caigny*
12 Model Town (as) a Collection of Scattered Architectural Forms
    Maarten Van Den Driessche
26 Communities of Practice: Reflections on a latter-day *tendens* in Flanders
    Irina Davidovici
40 Projects   *Louis De Mey and Dirk Somers*
144 *Capricci*
146 Building a Middle Ground, 9 Voices   *André Loeckx, Leo Van Broeck,
    Christian Rapp, Kristiaan Borret, Peter Vanden Abeele,
    Stefan Devoldere, Edith Wouters, Katrien Embrechts, Paul Vermeulen*

Memory as a Design Studio

Sofie De Caigny

The time when we could consume materials and space unthinkingly is far behind us. It is becoming increasingly important to deal carefully with the existing situation. This calls for a redefinition of the basic principles of design with memory coming into play more. This new direction manifests itself at all scale levels: from the narrative of the design via the choice of materials to urban planning figures and landscape design. The history of landscapes and places (both morphological and immaterial), of building and design traditions, of materials and ideas forms the frame of reference for new designs.

In the densely built-up landscape of Flanders and Brussels, this reversal of the basic principles of architecture is perhaps even more at issue than elsewhere in the world. A historically evolved fabric of small towns and paved roads and more than a century of land consumption without a clear urban planning framework to preserve the open space make the region one of the most densely populated in Europe. Housing, work, transport and leisure are spread over the territory without the spatial density of a metropolis. This nebular city encompasses villages and towns, like boulders or knots in a diffuse fabric. For several decades, architects and urban planners have been arguing for the densification and reinforcement of these centres to achieve a better balance between open space and built-up areas, and a better distribution of the benefits and burdens of public investments. The densification of centres will bring about a positive impact on water management, mobility, air quality and nature management.

The densification of centres also forces us to think about how these centres can be given shape architecturally. The configuration of the historically evolved towns and villages, their public buildings, dwellings, squares and streets bear the traces of layered social, economic and cultural developments. They show the changing relationship between individuals and the community, how newcomers found a place and how all aspects of life are constantly developing. They often have qualities that have accumulated over centuries. Any contemporary addition cannot but take a conscious attitude towards this stratification, and should add quality and meaning to it. For this, morphological, typological and tectonic analyses are necessary, but they should not prevent reinterpretations and the creative elaboration of a contemporary idiom.

For the seventeenth edition of the Architecture Biennale in Venice, the Flanders Architecture Institute launched a call for projects that addressed memory as a design studio innovatively. Out of more than 50 entries, a jury chose Bovenbouw Architectuur's *Composite Presence* project because it connects the reassessment of the discipline on the basis of 'what is already there' to the question of densification in a way that is interesting in architectural terms. *Composite Presence* shows a fictitious landscape of models of existing (and mostly realized) projects. Their arrangement shows the challenges of both densification and a careful architecture that, with varying strategies but always very precisely, deals with the existing situation.

The exhibition thus provides a very tangible answer to the question posed by Hashim Sarkis, curator of the 17th Architecture Biennale: 'How Will We Live Together?' With the outbreak of the pandemic, this question has acquired a new urgency. The health crisis raging on a global scale is challenging the existing social models. An accelerated digital revolution in the work life and in education makes the world even more present in a virtual manner than before. The boundaries between working and living are becoming increasingly blurred. At the same time, the quality of the local environment is gaining in importance because of the restrictions imposed on mobility in general and travel in particular. In this respect, Richard Sennett's[1] plea for diversity in city life, with a stratification of functions and good transitions between private and public places, is more topical than ever.

Composite Presence depicts the spatial basis for how this proper coexistence can take shape in Flanders and Brussels. It is a composition of buildings that

---

1   Sennett, R. (2018). *Building and Dwelling. Ethics for the City*. London: Allen Lane.

have been brought together in a new relation on a scale of 1:15. In reality, the projects are to be found in the city, in the outskirts and in village centres. With the projects, Bovenbouw is creating a new piece of the city. In this city, programmes such as healthcare, safety, trade, production and leisure alternate with housing. Gradual transitions between public and private suggest sufficient intimacy *and* a variety of places for public life. The selection includes new constructions as well as restoration and renovation projects. Together, they bring a historical stratification that also counts in reality and thus aptly demonstrate that the city of the future is not a distant utopia, but to a large extent exists already.

Dirk Somers of Bovenbouw Architectuur discusses the fictitious model landscape as a three-dimensional *capriccio* that makes it possible to physically experience the imagined city. To further explore the *capriccio,* he invited fellow architects to represent their vision of the future city in a new composition. These 45 *capricci* took the form of postcards of new cityscapes with both existing and unrealized buildings. As a whole, the postcards expressly show the coexistence of the different time layers in the European city and the way architects deal with this when designing the city of the future.

In this catalogue, Louis De Mey wrote short explanatory texts about each project in Bovenbouw's fictional landscape. These texts are accompanied by location plans that situate the projects in their actual context. This provides an insight into the whimsical plots that architects work with in Flanders and Brussels, and shows the close involvement with the surrounding fabric that this condition entails. The combination of De Mey's text with these plans shows the urban planning gesture that architectural projects in Flanders and Brussels necessarily require in the face of a historical lack of proper spatial planning.

In her contribution to this book, Irina Davidovici examines Bovenbouw's selection from the perspective of the 'tendenza' mechanism that she developed to understand the particular densification of architectural culture around Ticino in the late 1960s and 1970s. She wonders whether there are parallel dynamics at play to get a grip on the current architectural production in Flanders and Brussels. She recognizes in that production an internalization of the attention for typology, form, the everyday and the stratification of the city and history as shared values. She investigates whether there are professional, cultural and academic networks in which such a collectively supported discourse can unfold to produce a coherent architectural production. In doing so, she also incorporates the broader policy-related context that includes architecture as a cultural project for the community.

A large number of the projects selected by Bovenbouw came about through the direct or indirect intervention of a public body that helped steer the quality control of the project. For instance, municipal services acted as commissioning authorities to develop difficult plots in socially fragile parts of the city in a qualitative manner, because a broader vision of urban development underlay an assignment or because a project was awarded through the procedures of a city architect or the Flemish Government Architect. In the text 'Building a Middle Ground', Maarten Van Den Driessche, Dirk Somers and I brought together nine voices that are fulfilling the mediating process on quality in the field. In short statements, they provide insight into a number of underlying visions and challenges of how it is possible to build further the city of today and tomorrow. These nine voices from the field reinforce the idea of the 'tendenza' that Davidovici elaborates in her text.

Maarten Van Den Driessche's contribution shows how the exhibition *Composite Presence* can be understood through three cultural traditions. He first emphasizes the whimsical form of the plots where the projects are to be found. He points out the importance of typo-morphological analyses and of the genealogy of the Belgian landscape to be able to grasp why architecture also equals urban planning in this region. Secondly, he places the Bovenbouw project in a tradition of bringing together existing and unrealized projects in a new constellation that aims to show how a city is shaped by large urban figures and architectural ensembles. Lastly, Van Den Driessche situates *Composite Presence* in a longer history of architectural models and plastic models that play with texture, colour and expression. Because of their scale and elaboration, the models are intended as autonomous objects, which refer at the same time to a non-existent but achievable reality. The three references through which Van Den Driessche interprets *Composite Presence* at first glance seem somewhat removed from the directness of the question 'How Will We Live Together?'. However, Van Den Driessche convincingly shows that it is precisely in this critical distance that the space to engage with this question arises. After all, it is in the portals and balconies, the windows and tactile façades, and in the imagination of the public space that the suggestion of life reveals itself. For Bovenbouw, Sarkis's question is unmistakably an assignment for architecture.

Model Town (as) a Collection of Scattered Architectural Forms

'Societies and persons assemble themselves according to their own interpretations of absolute reference and traditional value; and, up to a point, collage accommodates both hybrid display and the requirements of self-determination.'[1]
—Colin Rowe

'The question is—a question which I might call a "political" question in the noblest sense of the word—whether we accept this breaking apart of cities and societies or whether we think that we can put the scattered elements back into a kind of unity.'[2]
—Alain Touraine

---

1   Rowe, C. and Koetter, F. (1978). *Collage City*. Cambridge, MA: MIT Press, pp. 144–145.

2   Alain Touraine, 'Die Stadt—ein überholter Entwurf?', as quoted in: Sieverts, T. (2003). *Cities Without Cities. An Interpretation of the Zwischenstadt*. London/New York: Spon Press, p. 54. See also: Touraine, A. (2013). *La Fin des sociétés*. Paris: Édition du Seuil / Point Essais.

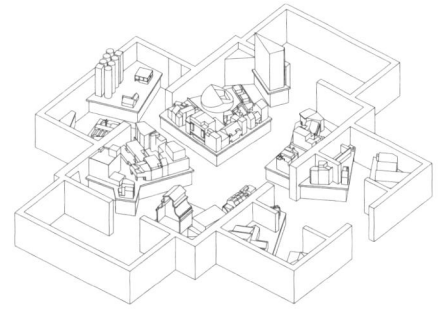

Axonometry of the Belgian pavilion,
Bovenbouw Architectuur

Maarten Van Den Driessche

High tables have been placed in the corners of the cruciform floor plan of the Belgian pavilion. Fifty models of recent architectural projects are arranged on the tables. The tabletops delimit different fields: larger and smaller surfaces, deep, narrow and long surfaces. Many tables have long, straight edges: different scale models are lined up in a row, forming a street frontage and thus suggesting that the individual projects are part of an urban ensemble. Most tabletops are shaped irregularly, however: titled, cut-off and considerably ill-defined. A first glance at the models emphasizes their heterogeneity. The collected architectural projects are very diverse in terms of character, size and scale. The majority consists of houses, but we also perceive smaller public facilities such as a school, a church, utilitarian infrastructure, office and industrial buildings. There are various new constructions, but also a large number of conversions and renovations. The particular care with which the texture, the colour and the articulation of the façades of the models has been rendered ultimately reinforces the composite and fragmentary character of the overall installation.

This text discusses not only the appearance of the scale model, but situates the exhibition proposal within a broader spatial and policy context in which the actual projects came about. After all, the model landscape creates a specific image of the architecture in Flanders and Brussels. It is not an objective reproduction of reality, but, following Louis Marin, a utopian construct: 'L'utopie réalise une intéressante équivalence entre son réferent—ce dont on parle, son project spécifique—et ses codes d'émission, de réception et de transmission'[3] (The utopia achieves an interesting equivalence between its referent—our subject, its specific project—and its codes of emission, reception and transmission). The model city establishes a specific relation between its referent—the architecture projects as they appear in reality—and the announced message—the way in which architecture production is discussed in the context of the Architecture

---

[3] Marin, L. (1973). *Utopiques: Jeux d'Espaces.* Paris: Les Éditions de Minuit, p. 24.

Biennale. Already with its borrowed title, *Composite Presence*, the exhibition is taking up a position with regard to the umbrella theme 'How Will We Live Together?'. The discursive embedding determines to a significant degree the extent to which the model installation will be read.

In this text I wish to point to three references which, as first associations, lay at the basis of the exhibition proposal. In this way, Marin's equivalency is partly decoded. A first section connects the typo-morphological analyses of Saverio Muratori with the genealogy of the Belgian landscape. The figurative power of Thomas Schütte's *Architekturmodellen* is then linked with the architectural diversity perceptible in the model landscape. This reference to the models of this post-conceptual visual artist makes clear how different activities and programmes are expressed via architecture. Lastly, the unencumbered appropriation of the compositional strategies and the contextualism in Colin Rowe's *Collage City* offers a basis on which to deal with formal heterogeneity, but also with brand-new architectural challenges. The three references recall a productive episode of theorization and reflection in the architectural discourse, where the *Sachlichkeit* of modernism makes way for a more layered architectural idiom.

À la manière de Saverio Muratori: the parcel and the form of the city

The overall installation is composed of projects that in fact are to be found at various places and are located in different geographies. Some buildings are situated in the nineteenth-century belt of city centres, others in the heart of small provincial towns. However, many buildings are set in the undefined suburban sprawl. Some projects fill a deep plot, others a broad one. Here building density

Recollecting Landscapes 6—De Haan
(Klemskerke), Driftweg, 22.09.2014

is sought upwards, there projects are grouped in rows. Freestanding objects are arranged meticulously on geometrically regular or rather incidental building plots. The way in which individual architects deal with contextual contingencies varies, but the parcel form repeatedly determines the building form. Despite the initial diversity, the different models are fitted together like pieces of a jigsaw puzzle.

The structural and structuring presence of individual parcels offers the first key to the reading of the model landscape.[4] Individual architecture projects relate to the form of the parcel and engage in a dialogue with their neighbours. The irregularity of the model tables is the consequence—and the direct representation—of the importance of the parcel, the urban fabric and, I wish to argue, of the genealogy of a territory in a state of transformation. The evolving process of urbanization is characterized by a particular dynamic in which landscape conditions, demographic evolutions, urban policy, built form and land use are closely interrelated.

With his meticulous analyses of historical cities such as Venice and Rome, Saverio Muratori reassessed the modernist paradigms of CIAM (Congrès Internationaux d'Architecture Moderne) and the accompanying technocratic planning logic. Muratori's theoretical work would be crucial for the Italian *Tendenza* movement and thus for the later work of Aldo Rossi, Ernesto Rogers, Vittorio Gregotti and Giorgio Grassi. The Italian morphological school showed itself to be sensitive to the stratification of the city, the qualities of vernacular architecture, the idea of organic growth, and historical continuity: 'The essential fact of urbanism is the organism and character of the city, the original sense of the development of its plan over time, of its collocation in the landscape, of its urban and building structures, its civic and social life, its moral climate, its traditions and history'.[5] On the basis of morphological studies of, among others, Venice (1959), the Italian architect pointed to the structural interconnectednes between the underlying topographical and geological structure and the successive transformations of the

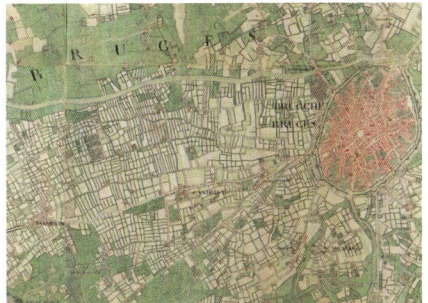

Territory of the Austrian Netherlands, Brugghe, 1771–1778, Joseph de Ferraris, KBR

4   I refer among others to an earlier text about school architecture: Van Den Driessche, M. (2016). 'The School Building as Urban Project. Coupling—Entity—Type—Fragment' in: Grafe, C. (ed.). *Flanders Architectural Review N°12*. pp. 63–70. See also the design research project 'Collectief wonen in een collectief landschap' conducted by a mixed team made up of Bovenbouw Architectuur and UGent's Labo A and LaboS: Swinnen, P. (2013). *Pilootprojecten Collectief Wonen*. Brussels: Flemish Government Architect.

5   Saverio Muratori (1946), *La valutazione dell' opera architettonica, posthumous publication*, Marinucci G. (ed.). (1980). Rome: Centro Studi di Storia Urbanistica, p. 258—as translated in Maretto, M. (2015). *Saverio Muratori: Il progetto della città | A Legacy in Urban Design*. Milan: Franco Angeli, p. 20.

built fabric. If we characterize the fine-meshed parcel structure in the exhibition proposal as structuring, then we must, *à la* Muratori, look closely at the connection between underlying topographical structure and construction form.

To fully understand the spatial challenges facing the region, it is useful to sketch briefly the particular genealogy of the Belgian urban landscape. The Ferraris maps make up a first starting point for this. This famous mapping operation carried out between 1771 and 1778 and consisting of some 200 sheets was created under Austrian tutelage. The atlas holds as one of the comprehensive mappings in Belgium and even Western Europe. It shows premodern Belgium under the Ancien Régime. In historical cities, we can see how development takes shape in an interplay between meandering watercourses and human interventions. But in the countryside too we can see the formative logic of individual parcels, which are indicated with canals, hedges and rows of trees. The delta of the Low Countries has had fertile soils since time immemorial. A finely ramified system of rivers and streams traverses the cities as well as the surrounding hinterland. The Ferraris sheets show at first sight a clear distinction between city and countryside. The cities lie enclosed within their walls and stand out as perfect geometric figures in relation to the hinterland. It seems as though culture and nature (the red and green fields on the map) have been placed opposite to each other as figure and ground.

This distinction appears to be less sharp than at first sight, however, especially if we consider the Ferraris maps from the perspective of today's land use. The current drawing of the territory is more layered, the land use is read in a more hybrid manner, and in a sense the clear-cut distinction between city and hinterland has become meaningless. At the start of the nineteenth century, the city walls were razed in countless towns to make room for working-class neighbourhoods, factories and railway infrastructure that connected the towns

A Land Never, Belgian contribution to
the 13th Venice Biennale by
AWJGGRAUaDVVTAT, Studio Joost Grootens

with one another along the riverbeds. Backed by an anti-urban subsidy policy, the city sprawled out from the second half of the twentieth century like an oil stain.[6] The rural parcels were further parcelled out. The areas that were green in the historical maps became increasingly red, in the sense that the patchwork of fertile farmlands that were intended for agricultural activities were now being colonized by suburban extensions. These extramural expansions of the city grafted themselves onto the underlying rural structure that, stimulated by land speculation and an urge to parcellize, was being increasingly fragmented.

The current urbanization process is characterized by a dual movement. The far-reaching development of the countryside is the direct consequence of the historical housing policy, political laissez-faire, the privatization of land, and failing government control. On the other hand, countermovement has taken place in recent years in the form of a renewed reflection on the city and urbanity. The importance of increased density, the proximity and mixture of functions, more optimal ground use were propagated in recent years as crucial policy challenges. The exhibition proposal integrates these two antagonistic narratives almost seamlessly. The radicalness of the proposal therefore lurks in the unexpected juxtaposition. No distinction is made in the installation as a whole between urban and rural environments. For instance, the Social House seems like an extension of the town hall in Langemark in the Westhoek—a region in Flanders that has been subject to demographic shrinkage in recent decades—appears alongside terraced houses in the nineteenth-century belt of Brussels, Ghent and Antwerp—which, on the contrary, have grown significantly in recent years. The resulting image is utopian. The model is a reflection of reality, but equally a fictionalizing commentary on this reality. The evocation of an organically grown, almost mythical medieval small town contrasts explicitly with a territorial condition that can no longer be described on the basis of a purely urban logic.

---

6   De Meulder, B., Schreurs, J., Cock, A., & Notteboom, B. (1999). Sleutelen aan het Belgische Stadslandschap. *Consumptie en territorium*, OASE, (52), pp. 78–113.

Volumetric disparities in
the valley of the Dender, 2006

À la manière de Thomas Schütte:
Bühne, shed, *huis, belvédère*

The curators retained strict control of the material reproduction of the architectural projects on display. Meticulously made wooden models were assembled with glue. All models were manufactured uniformly on a scale of 7:100. The models are large and are prominently present in the exhibition hall. The colouring, the materials used or rich textures have been imitated with stratified wooden panels, carved surfaces, paint layers and additional fine pencil drawings. Although the models are utterly architectonic, they are atypical architectural models. This effect is not only a consequence of the equal treatment imposed explicitly on the projects that apparently erases individual authorship, but is due even more to the fact that the model-like character of the manufactured artefacts has been emphasized. The way in which the models have been fabricated accentuates the mimetic relation between the model and the reproduced building.

The use of wooden tables as socles, the improper scale that makes it possible to introduce detail and the explicit materialization bring to mind the work of German artist Thomas Schütte, a second reference which we here wish to specify briefly. Thomas Schütte is considered one of the protagonists of the renowned *Kunstakademie* in Düsseldorf. Schütte reintroduced in his artistic oeuvre notions such as craftsmanship, pictorial subjectivity and expressive power. This was his way of reacting to the then widespread diffusion of conceptual art and the institutional critique. 'Fundamentally my works almost always have the character of a proposal and first exist in model form, in order to be then realized, or not.'[7] Monumental architectural models were the medium par excellence by which the artist could explore the narrative, figurative and imaginative ability of his artistic output.

---

7   Hentschel, M. 'Binnen en buiten. Thomas Schütte in gesprek met Martin Hentschel (februari 1987)' in: Loock, U. (ed.). (1990). *Thomas Schütte*. Bern/Paris/Eindhoven: Kunsthalle Bern/ARC—Musée d'Art Moderne de la Ville de Paris/ Stedelijk Van Abbemuseum, p. 82.

Landhaus 4 (1986), *Studio II* (1983) and *Studio I* (1983), Thomas Schütte, Collection Herbert Foundation, Ghent

Schütte's sculptural models refer explicitly to architecture, but still retain their autonomy as visual artefacts. A first series of so-called *Architekturmodelle* was made in the context of the art manifestation *Westkunst* in 1980. Schütte designed three monumental 'total installations' for this group exhibition. However, for programmatic and budgetary reasons, these were never carried out. The artist then presented the designs together in model form. 'The work was made in wood and on a scale of 1:5: a *Schiff* of 90 × 200 × 100 cm, a *Kiste* of 110 × 200 × 100 cm, and a *Bühne* of 120 × 250 × 100 cm. So Schütte made models measuring about one metre high and up to 2.5 metres long.'[8] The formal analogy between the model installation in the Belgian pavilion and this canonical artwork is unambiguous.

The installation for the Belgian pavilion includes three smaller architectural projects that detach themselves from the parcel structure but can also distinguish themselves from the other models on account of their smaller scale. They look like *objets trouvés* or, in reference to Koetter and Rowe's treaty, 'stimulants for the urban collage'.[9] It concerns a small watchtower by Baeten Hylebos Architecten commissioned by the Baudelo Foundation that manages some delicate nature areas in the Waasland; the conversion of a chapel in Muizen that was turned into a hang-out for the young by PULS; and the pavilion De Nor by FVWW and the artist Dennis Tyfus in the Middelheim Museum in Antwerp. The three smaller projects play on three different dimensions of architectural representation. The wooden deer tower serves as a *belvédère*. It is a watchtower that offers views over an untouched area of natural landscape. By clustering high white benches around the religious relic, PULS architecten turned the site of the chapel into a shelter where residents can temporarily withdraw from the public sphere into the seclusion of a *hortus conclusus* (enclosed garden). The installation in the open-air museum was literally conceived as a *Bühne* (stage) and refers most explicitly

[8] A nice article on this early work of Thomas Schütte: Vervoort, S. (2015). '"Iets ontbreekt": neoavantgarde en traditie in het vroege werk van Thomas Schütte' in: *De Witte Raaf*, 30 (178), pp. 11–16.

[9] Rowe, C. and Koetter, F. *Collage City*, pp. 172–177, See also: Dercon, C. (ed.). (1990). *Theatergarden Bestiarum. The Garden as Theater as Museum.* Cambridge, MA: MIT Press.

De Nor, FVWW architecten in collaboration with Dennis Tyfus

to the work of Thomas Schütte. The formal similarity between De Nor and Schütte's *Schiff* is striking. The concrete stage with a drawing by Tyfus and the bunker-like stand articulates a place where the contemporary artist organizes musical and artistic performances during the summer. The neon sign that reads De Nor (The nick), like many titles in Schütte's oeuvre, adds an additional, absurdist connotation to the structure.

The model city is primarily composed of expressive façades. The model landscape does not offer a look at the intimate private life of its inhabitants; or rather, we only get to see a glimpse of that life. The interiors have only been developed minimally and in no way show signs of having been taken over by domestic life—unlike, for instance, doll's houses.[10] And yet the exposed buildings demonstrate character. Distinctive, figurative elements demand attention. The focus lies on the composition of the façade, portals and entrance halls, on balconies, winter gardens and bay windows, plinths and cornices. There are the flights of steps that appear prominently in the façade and that stage movements throughout the house. There are displays and glass shop fronts that sporadically offer us a view into the lobby of a public building or invite us to enter the building. It is the physiognomy of the façade that expresses the complex whole of architectural programmes and thus the human activities that lie concealed behind them.

Most of the reproduced architecture projects consist of houses, but the model does not show an exclusive residential landscape. After all, cities are not just where people live, but also where goods are produced and trade is conducted; where services are provided and guests are received. The city must be governed, and safety must be ensured—there are no fewer than two police stations—but the city must also care for children and its most vulnerable residents. People come together in buildings for several reasons, and therefore different degrees of openness and

---

10 On the motif of the doll's house, see: Somers, D. and Van Den Driessche, M. 'A Conversation Between Friends' in: Somers, D., De Caigny, S., Van Den Driessche, M. and Verschaffel, B. (2019). *Bovenbouw Architectuur. Living the Exotic Everyday.* Antwerp: VAi, pp. 190–202 (especially p. 191).

Chapel of Our Lady of the Muizenhoek, PULS architecten

intimacy must be articulated via the façade. In this case, the façade does not form a strict division between private and public sphere, but mediates between both.

Schütte's *Westkunstmodelle*, but also the architecture projects discussed above, articulate very different registers to deal with the public character of architecture: exposure to the public in the case of the theatrical scene, or rather private withdrawal in the case of the shelter, and the many gradations between these two extreme positions. The pronounced façades with all their detail, their inscriptions, colours, textures, give a face—the Latin word *faces*—to the life that unfolds in the urban interiors. Architecture creates not only space to be used, architecture also acts as a layered signifier. Architecture uses recognizable architectural forms, signals and symbols to communicate to the public about the building's character.

À la manière de Colin Rowe: architectural negotiations at this juncture

Lastly, the third reference is the most explicit, but at the same time the least clear to construe. The title of the total installation refers after all to the famous drawing by Hans Kollhoff and David Griffith that featured as the frontispice to Fred Koetter and Colin Rowe's *Collage City* from 1978. The drawing shows an enigmatic collection of architectural fragments that suggest an idea of an urban space in a loose composition against a white background. We recognize in the plan drawing some monumental figures, such as the elliptic plan of the iconic *Piazza dell'Anfiteatro di Luca* that is crocheted up to the urban fabric around the equally monumental Uffizi Gallery in Florence. The enigmatic drawing is an interpretation of and continuation of cartographic material made by illustrious predecessors such as Piranesi's *Campo Marzio* from 1762 or, a bit more recently, the collage map *Città Analoga*

Observation tower,
Baeten Hylebos Architecten

(Analogous City) from 1976, by Aldo Rossi, Bruno Reichlin, Fabio Reinhart and Eraldo Consolascio, which took shape at ETH Zürich as a collective project and was brought into circulation in different capacities.[11] Like the drawing of Griffith and Kollhoff, the group around Aldo Rossi collected a heterogeneous collection of real and imaginary projects that stem from a disparate set of geographical locations. Despite the clear differences, they all show how the city can take shape through monumental urban figures and powerful architectural ensembles.

In Koetter and Rowe's treaty, the collage is presented as a critique of the modernist planning tradition. In their manifesto, urban planning fit-in exercises are executed as a counter-project of the modernist *tabula rasa*. The assembled city is the very opposite of Le Corbusier's *Plan Voisin:* his devastating project for Paris. The collage technique is described in the work as a 'democratic' strategy to involve very different cultural impulses and historical eras together. For Rowe, assembling urban fragments and fitting them together was in the first place a formalist and self-referential action, which had to be stripped of any ideological claim. As with Rowe's contemporaries Léon and Rob Krier, he was not averse to a nostalgic reflex. Rowe's compositions with their interrupted symmetry axes and figurative urban forms are characterized by nostalgia for the exuberant baroque urban planning or the beaux-arts tradition. The collage thus served just as much as an alibi to compose urban entities with grand, almost despotic gestures and with a not-unproblematic aristocratic erudition.[12]

The formal operation underlying this curatorial project is undoubtedly indebted to Rowe's theoretical project; yet the founding premise is very different. Today too, the field of tension between the employed reference and the depicted reality is a crucial key articulating this difference. The overall layout of the model installation does not start after all with the urban figure or the urbanistic gesture, but manifests itself by means of individual architecture projects that have been

---

11   Szacka, L.-C. (2018). 'Città Analoga: Aldo Rossi's Visual Theory on Display' in: Miljacki, A. and Lawrence, A.R. (eds.). *Terms of Appropriation: Modern Architecture and Global Exchange*. London: Routledge, pp. 263–277.

12   Ockman, J. (1998). 'Form Without Utopia: Contextualizing Colin Rowe' in *Journal of the Society of Architectural Historians*, 57 (4), pp. 448–456.

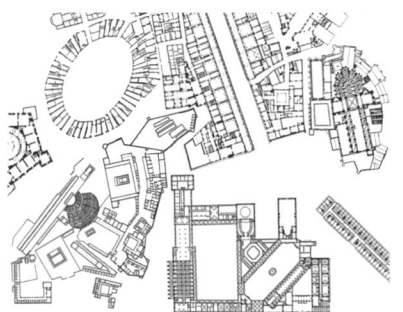

City of Composite Presence, 1976, David Griffin and Hans Kollhoff

assembled in a well-thought manner, yet more or less form an urban whole on arbitrary grounds. In the current sociopolitical order, the architect hardly has any control over the complex territorial conditions, property structures and land use, and this is not in the least the argument. The underlying urban structure is not the actual object of the model installation on display. The existing urban environment forms the reality which the designer needs to relate to, rather than the intentional result of planning processes or top-down design actions.

The projects on display are the result—and the representation—of a changed architecture policy. All projects emerged in the context of a specific cultural policy that created the right conditions to give high-quality architecture a chance. All the projects on display emerged under the impulse of a rich institutional field.[13] Today, different authorities accompany the realization of high-quality architecture projects. The intervention of countless public actors was a decisive criterion in the selection of separate architecture projects in this installation. With regard to the almost absent architecture policy three decades ago, this architecture policy in Flanders and Brussels initiated a genuine culture shift. Today, architecture is taking shape within all sorts of 'quality chambers' where private parties and public actors negotiate architectural quality and the meaning of buildings.[14] The obvious architectural diversity is a direct consequence of these truly 'democratic' negotiation procedures.

The current age poses many new challenges that cannot simply be tackled with a historically handed-down formula. Alain Touraine, with whose motif we opened the text, has described the disruptive impact of the current economic order in different texts. Globalization processes, the widely disseminated mobility, the flexibilization of the working life in our services and network economy, so his argument goes, have a far-reaching influence on the organization of our everyday life.[15] These external conditions lead moreover to a far-reaching spatial detachment.

---

13   Van Den Driessche, M. (2020). 'Architecture in Flanders: A Quick Scan' in: *Flanders Architectural Review N°14: When Attitudes Take Form*, pp. 9–28.

14   See the contribution further in this book 'Building a Middle Ground, 9 Voices', pp. 146–168.

15   Touraine, A. (2013). *La fin des sociétés*, p. 657.

A competition proposal in
Atelier Bouwmeester, Brussels, 2012

How we live is organized differently and influences in turn how we see the city. We are in contact with others without professional and relational activities explicitly having to take place explicitly in a physical or metropolitan space. Familial, professional and social bonds take on other forms. Today we cherish other expectations with regard to the tie to our domicile, the idea of a home and therefore also the meaning of architecture. This explains in part why old dichotomies—such as between city and countryside, the functional division between housing, work and leisure, or between powerful urban figures and the anonymous, vernacular urban fabric—are losing in relevance. The societal evolutions mentioned also explain the heterogeneous appearance of the model installation. In the current political and economic circumstances, the collage—and more generally the composite character of the architectural composition—has a different role and meaning than in Rowe's manifesto. It is a way of cleverly dealing with the available conditions rather than the formalist expression of the postmodern zeitgeist or the expression of a retrograde, traditionalist attitude.

Despite important ecological challenges that the climate problem or the colonization of the countryside entail, two themes that are here addressed only indirectly, a progressive force manifests itself in the installation. Maintaining, refurbishing and adapting the existing heritage are also expressions of sustainable management and design, and can be equally innovative.[16] Together with the protection of open landscape areas, dealing with the existing heritage, according to Thomas Sieverts, is one of the most important cultural challenges: 'The handling of multifarious disused spaces, revaluations, interpretation of disused resources all become important planning tasks, and they are to a large extent essentially cultural tasks.'[17] Neither the traditional urban planning tools nor the technocratic zeal for regulation are adequate to accompany the transformation of buildings and urban fragments that have fallen into disuse or received a new social destination.

---

16   In that sense, the project fits in a more long-term agenda of the Flanders Architecture Institute. See: Grafe, C. (2011). *Vlugschrift Dierbaar is duurzaam. Zes stellingen rond architectuur, cultuur en ecologie*. Antwerp: VAi; Grafe, C. and De Caigny, S. (2017). *Onvoltooid verleden*. Antwerp: VAi.

17   Sieverts, T. (2003). *Cities Without Cities. An Interpretation of the Zwischenstadt*, p. 81.

The model advocates an approach in which fine-meshed architectural operations take centre stage, and reuse, reconstruction, extension, reparation and modernization of the existing heritage are given a real chance. The architecture on display emerged in reaction to contextual givens and locally anchored negotiation procedures. All projects were reactions to new social questions or to found qualities in the existing landscaping morphology. The model installation shows that grandiose urban planning gestures are not exclusively determining for the shape of the city. Coherence can be found through subtle architectural interventions in the fine grain of the urban fabric. The resulting landscape is the appealing evocation of an organically grown and composite city.

The model installation calls on the cultural imagination, but also relativizes the ambition to systematically opt for radical overthrow and the latest sociopolitical project. This text took Louis Marin's definition of the utopia as its basis. The 'play of spaces', as Marin would subtitle his book about utopian thought, labelled the French theorist as utopian. Clearly this definition of utopia differs strongly from Rowe's definition with which he criticized the sociopolitical aspirations of the modernist project. Marin's semiological analysis of the particular narrative structure of More's *Utopia* shows that stories and representations, such as sign and referent, establish an imaginary relation to reality. We showed that the model on display is a critical and studious reflection of the reality that the model represents. The utopia is in this case a project of cultural imagination, but by no means a politico-totalitarian project. The model landscape celebrates the heterogeneity of contemporary architecture in Flanders. The assemblage of architecture fragments presents itself not only as an inevitable condition, however, but also proves itself to be a potential that can be seized. The scale model—and the reality it refers to—can in that sense also be seen as a thought figure that could be imitated in dealing with future challenges.

Brussels #1, 1997

Communities of Practice:
Reflections on a latter-day *tendens* in Flanders

For Christian Kieckens, 1951–2020

Irina Davidovici

Synthetic cities

The Bovenbouw installation in the Belgian pavilion brings to mind a perpetually reimagined Venice—an archipelago of architectural fragments, structured as much by the islands as by the open space between them. Through fictional proximity, the 50 projects bring to visibility a collective artistic stance within a common regional and historical index. Their juxtaposition makes visible the shared cultural and professional backgrounds of the recent architecture in Flanders and Brussels, revealing the existence of social and political frameworks that underwrite the formal heterogeneity of the exhibits. At the same time, the constructed urbanity of the formats declares affinities with a Western theoretical discourse. It reflects upon Aldo Rossi's notion of the city as a collective mnemonic device, the synthetic 'politics of bricolage' beneath Colin Rowe and Fred Koetter's *Collage City* (1978) and its inset collage *City of Composite Presence* by Hans Kollhoff and David Griffin (whose name, initially borrowed from Rowe's text, lends itself to the current installation). These 'cities of the mind', to paraphrase Rowe once more, are themselves inscribed in the older tradition of Canaletto and Marlowe's *capricci*, which relocated the Palladian monuments of Vicenza, and more idiosyncratically London's St Paul's Cathedral, in imaginary projections of Venice, identifiable by the replacement of solid streets with liquid, reflective foregrounds.

The Canaletto and Marlowe in question were held up by Rowe as conceptual precedents of Collage City.[1] In them, viewers recognize actual buildings as fragments and actual cities as stage sets, brought together in an alternative reality articulated by tradition and utopia. Thus, the Bovenbouw installation positions itself in a series of synthetic cities that have permeated the Western architectural imagination for centuries, 'for, fundamentally, the city of composite presence is too pervasive an idea ever to become outdated'.[2] Ungrounded, dislocated,

1 Rowe, C. and Koetter, F. (1981). *Collage City*. Cambridge, MA: MIT Press, pp. 178–180.

2 Rowe, C. and Koetter, F. (1981). *Collage City*, p. 181.

the Flemish projects too find themselves displaced and recomposed into a perpetually reimagined floating city. Their shared basis is not merely regional or historical, but primarily intellectual.

Collective affinities

Historically, shared affinities in artistic and architectural productions have often emerged in specific cultural basins at certain times, circulating elsewhere to create trajectories and genealogies of ideas. In the last 50 years, this kind of recurring phenomena has been denoted by a vague and usually contested terminology. Despite its inherent problematic (since borders do not stop cultural influences), the regional or national index offers a seemingly clear criterion for collective definitions. This gives rise to umbrella terms as popular as they are misleading, often combining the qualification of novelty ('new', 'recent', 'contemporary', 'emerging'), regional and cultural attributes (Italian / Ticinese / Por-tuguese / Belgian / Flemish / Spanish / London / New York / Swiss), and collective nouns (architecture / school / group / etc.). The meaning of such composites is understandably unstable from one decade to the next, since nothing is forever 'new', regional denominations are viewed with suspicion, and 'schools' or 'groups' are often external projections resisted from within. Terminologies that specify the historical context offer a welcome precision, even though the Flemish 'Generation '74' (referring to the vintage year of Sint-Lucas Ghent graduates) and the 'Swiss architects born around 1950' (self-explanatory, but mostly referring to the generation of Jacques Herzog and Pierre de Meuron, Roger Diener, Marcel Meili, Christian Sumi and Marianne Burkhalter, etc.) end up referring to contemporaneous parallel architecture cultures.

More resilient, albeit notoriously vague, are the euphemistic terms: *la tendenza,* the 'grays', the 'whisperers', *les silencieux*.[3] Such terms denote historically specific regional clusters of critically inclined architects, operating at a high level of intellectual and creative intensity. And yet these names are seldom given by the participants themselves; rather, they tend to signal their newly found relevance in the international discourse. The various modes of practice they denote share a strong element of reflection, manifested in a written production parallel to the built: essays, monographs, exhibitions. Another feature is their collaborative aspect: these are not ad hoc groupings of isolated individuals, but people producing and exchanging knowledge in shared professional and academic networks. A typical example of such collaborative, reflective endeavours are group exhibitions. The gathering and comparison of contemporaneous works and practitioners creates a momentum for articulating shared theoretical platforms, which lead to the emergence of collective group awareness.[4] (In the case of the current exhibit in the Belgian pavilion, the Bovenbouw installation follows in a tradition of group exhibitions established in the 1980s, more specifically the 1991 Venice Biennale installation conceived by Marc Dubois and designed by Christian Kieckens, in which heterogeneous projects were presented against a neutral common background of wall-mounted pedestals in simple materials.[5])

The various *tendenze* since the 1960s are not stylistic schools. Rather, they are geographically disparate manifestations of a shared predisposition. By *tendenza* I mean in the first place the collectively coherent production of a group of artists at a certain time and place. The common theme that runs through the succession of *tendenze* is the careful gaze upon the past and the everyday. This places them in a curious tension with the architectural avant-garde which, in a traditional sense, perpetually articulates a fictional future, alternatively shiny and dystopian. By contrast, these *arrière-gardes* find inspiration in the grit of the present, support

---

[3] Christophe Van Gerrewey refers to the silent generation in his book: Van Gerrewey, C. (2014). *Architectuur in België. 25 jaar in 75 projecten.* Tielt: Lannoo, p. 8.

[4] For the case of recent Belgian Flemish architecture culture, see: De Caigny, S. and Vandermarliere, K. (2016). 'More than Punctual Interventions: Cultural Events, Competitions and Public Debate as Impetus for Architectural Culture in Flanders, 1974–2000' in: De Caigny, S. et al. (eds.). *Autonomous Architecture in Flanders: The Early Works of Marie-José van Hee, Christian Kieckens, Marc Dubois, Paul Robbrecht and Hilde Daem.* Leuven: Leuven University Press, pp. 49–61.

[5] See: Sterken, S. (2016). 'Ghostwriters of the Young Flemish Architecture: Marc Dubois, Christian Kieckens and the Architecture Museum Foundation, 1983–1992' in: De Caigny, S. et al. (eds.). *Autonomous Architecture in Flanders*, pp. 76–87.

in the historical past, and creativity in the ordinary. This predilection amounts to a common methodological platform, repeatedly articulated in historically disparate, yet conceptually related, 'gentle manifestos'.[6] Their reflectivity engenders a design method based on the interpretation of everyday realities 'as found'; architecture results from the subtle transformation of existing cultural conditions. The corresponding design method sounds by now familiar to most practitioners and students of architecture. It comprises the analysis of cultural, typological, material, morphological layers of reality, and their synthesis in architectural form. If the built results differ, it is because they replicate different formal and material conditions, shaped by the cultures in which the architecture is situated. So what, then, of the current 50 projects in the Belgian pavilion? What is their status in this recent tradition? Can they be seen as the manifestation of a *tendens* in Flanders?

Tendenze in perpetual translation

Considering the continuities at play, it is no surprise that the same *Capriccio* by Canaletto that shored up Rowe's plea for *Collage City* had earlier illustrated Aldo Rossi's seminal text 'L'architettura della raggione come architettura di tendenza' (1969).[7] Rossi first postulated the notion of *tendenza* in the context of the locally defined exhibition *Illuminismo e architettura del Settecento Veneto*. And yet the historical, indeed, regional circumstances of this occurrence mattered little to Rossi. He defined *tendenza* as a shared 'stylistic will' (*volontà di stile*) manifest in the production of eighteenth-century Veneto artists and architects:

> … stylistic will that enables one to analyse forms and the world of forms so as to arrive at an autonomous construct. This conception of

---

6 First used by Robert Venturi in *Complexity and Contradiction* (1966), the 'gentle manifesto' recently re-emerged in: Somers, D. and Van Den Driessche, M. (2019). 'A Conversation Between Friends' in: Somers, D., Van Den Driessche, M. and Verschaffel, B. *Bovenbouw Architectuur. Living the Exotic Everyday*. Antwerp: VAi, pp. 145–202.

7 Rossi, A. (1969). 'L'architettura della raggione come architettura di tendenza' in: Brusatin, M. (ed.). *Illuminismo e architettura del '700 [Settecento] Veneto: Catalogo della mostra, 31 Agosto–9 Novembre 1969*. Venice: Castelfranco Veneto, pp. 7–15.

art as pure speculation on appearance, as research into the existent forms of architecture, opens one of the most important avenues of modern art. Moreover, this combination of architectural objects, forms, materials is meant to create a potential reality of unexpected developments ... to construct the real.[8]

Moving freely between historical commentary and theoretical proposition, Rossi explored the notion of *tendenza* as a perennial condition, potentially applicable in understanding and cataloguing contemporary work. The term itself had earlier appeared in a 1946 *Domus* article by Ernesto Rogers, revisited in the *Casabella* essay 'Elogio della tendenza' in 1958.[9] In the original sense, *tendenza* was associated with the cultivation of historical conscience, the deliberate pursuit of cultural continuity. For an artist's oeuvre to be coherent, Rogers argued, it was necessary for it to circumscribe a defined intellectual position, supported by a consistent cultural and moral horizon. *Tendenza* was the act of translating between layers, of connecting them, and making them visible in a stylistic sense.[10] Crucially, while *tendenza* belonged to a personal artistic enterprise, in order to be relevant and truly critical, it had to engage with its cultural context. 'To speak of *tendenza*', Rogers concluded, 'is an act of modesty that integrates the activity of each individual into the culture of their epoch'.[11]

By defining *tendenza* as *volontà di stile*, Rossi associated it more explicitly with its stylistic manifestations. In the early 1970s, the notion shifted to its currently accepted use of *La Tendenza*. Coupled with the definite article, it morphed into a historical artistic movement, primarily associated with the abstract typological forays of neo-rationalist Northern Italian architects (Rossi, Vittorio Gregotti, Giorgio Grassi, Massimo Scolari). The programmatic platform of *La Tendenza* was thematized during the 15th Milan Triennale in 1973, when

---

8   Rossi, A. (1969). 'L'architettura della raggione come architettura di tendenza', p. 9. Author's translation into English.

9   Rogers, E. (1958). 'Elogio della tendenza' in: Rogers, E. (1997). *Esperienza dell'architettura*. Milan: Skira, pp. 88–90.

10   Rogers, E. (1958). 'Elogio della tendenza', republished in French translation in: Mazzoni, C. (ed.) (2013). *La tendenza. Une avant-garde architecturale italienne, 1950–1980*. Marseilles: Parenthèses, p. 90.

11   Rogers, E. (1958). 'Elogio della tendenza', p. 92. Author's translation into English.

its meaning became firmly associated with the project of architectural autonomy. As Massimo Scolari wrote in 1973:

> For the *Tendenza*, architecture is a cognitive process that in and of itself, in the acknowledgment of its own autonomy, is today necessitating a refounding of the discipline; that refuses interdisciplinary solutions to its own crisis; that does not pursue and immerse itself in political, economic, social, and technological events only to mask its own creative and formal sterility, but rather desires to understand them so as to be able to intervene in them with lucidity.[12]

The notion of *tendenza* was shortly to skip borders and languages with the occasion of another architectural exhibition, this one in Switzerland. The influential group show *Tendenzen—Neuere Architektur im Tessin*, held in Zurich in 1975, brought the Ticino architecture of the late 1960s and early 1970s to a Northern Swiss audience still enthralled by Rossi's charismatic teaching at ETH between 1972 and 1974.[13] The exhibition established a new generation of Italian-Swiss architects nationally and internationally, putting Ticino on the map of architectural destinations for at least two decades. And yet this phenomenon was deeply indebted to theoretical and methodological import from Italy. The plural German form of the title, *Tendenzen*, fulfilled a double role, acknowledging the translation potential of Italian theory into Swiss and other productions while at the same time recognizing the intrinsic heterogeneity of the Ticinese positions. The writings of several participants collected in the catalogue demonstrated the extent to which they replicated the main theoretical foci of *La Tendenza*: the claims of history and the city, the use of typology and morphology as design methods, the focus on architectural form. Moreover, the exhibited buildings were framed by

---

12   Quoted in: Hays, K. M. (ed.). (1998). *Architectural Theory since 1968*. Cambridge, MA: MIT Press, pp. 131–132.

13   See: Moravánszky, Á. and Hopfengärtner, J. (eds.). (2011). *Aldo Rossi und die Schweiz: Architektonische Wechselwirkungen*. Zurich: gta Verlag.

a sophisticated theoretical reading, projected from outside by the curator Martin Steinmann. His essay in the exhibition catalogue, 'Reality as History. Notes for a Discussion of Realism in Architecture', placed the 'new Ticinese architecture' under the sign of autonomy as the only unifying, 'essential common denominator'.[14] Its reproduction in international publications in the following years signalled its disconnection from the claims of any particular place. Autonomy thus became a transgressive theme, subsuming the heterogeneous forms, design approaches and cultural claims under one theoretical construct with general validity.

Reflective practitioners: towards a *tendens* in Belgium

The theme of autonomy re-emerged in the historiography of recent architecture in Flanders, starting with the *Autonomous Architecture* publication on the so-called Generation '74, a reference to Marie-José Van Hee, Christian Kieckens, Marc Dubois, Paul Robbrecht and Hilde Daem, who all graduated from the Sint-Lucas school of architecture in Ghent in 1974.[15] Belgian architect Caroline Voet identified the common grounds of their approach as 'the study of historical references'—a multilayered 'fluctuating signature' that 'brought a blend of Venturi, Wittkower and Norberg-Schulz to Flanders'.[16] Dirk Somers, principal of Bovenbouw, qualifies the influence of Robert Venturi, Denise Scott-Brown and Steve Izenour on Belgian architecture culture, depicting Flanders as particularly receptive to ideas they had developed. One ground for this affinity, in Somers' reading, was their positioning of architectural references in the grey area between high and popular culture, whereas 'what passes for Pop Art in Belgium makes use of the local commonplace, rather than the flamboyant iconography of American consumer culture'.[17] At a yet more fundamental level,

---

14 Steinmann, M. (1976). 'Reality as History. Notes for a Discussion of Realism in Architecture' in: Boga, T. and Steinmann, M. (eds.). *Tendenzen. Neuere Architektur im Tessin* (2nd ed.). Zurich: ETHZ Organisationsstelle für Ausstellungen des Institutes GTA, p. 155. English translation in original.

15 See: 'Timelines' in: De Caigny, S. et al. (eds.). (2016). *Autonomous Architecture in Flanders*, pp. 213–221.

16 Voet, C. (2016). 'Architecture between Dwelling and Spatial Systematics. The Early Works of the Generation of '74' in: De Caigny, S. et al. (eds.). *Autonomous Architecture in Flanders*, p. 118.

17 *Ibid.*

their work exemplified a strategy of sharp architectural interventions bringing order to convoluted or ambivalent situations. 'A very Belgian reading of Venturi', Somers muses, 'legitimises architecture as a play on reality. The solitary Belgian architect arms himself/herself with Venturi and presents himself/herself as a practical strategist that does not address inherent contradictions, but converts them into enthralling signs'.[18] This attitude vis-à-vis inherited reality comes into its own in the critique of Belgium's disjointed urban context, in which strategic architectural interventions take a corrective role by inserting an autonomous order of their own: 'the vacuum created by dysfunctional urban development is repaired by architectural discipline'.[19]

The question of architectural autonomy has long troubled architects, especially those of various *tendenza* stripes. Pier Vittorio Aureli pointed out that autonomy does not involve the 'strategic retreat' of architecture from its sociopolitical and historical circumstances.[20] One origin for the term was 1960s Venice, where IUAV hosted an informal network of architects that preferred theorizing about architecture and the city to a pragmatic submission to professional limitations. Another source was again Rossi, for whom, in Aureli's reading:

> ... autonomy entailed a refusal not of the reality of the emerging post-industrial city, but of the techno-utopian visions of the contemporary world ... For Rossi the possibility of autonomy occurred as a possibility of theory: of the reconstruction of the political, social, and cultural significations of urban phenomena divorced from any technocratic determinism.[21]

Parallel to Venturi although ideologically distinct, the works and writings of Northern Italian thinkers and practitioners in the 1960s and 1970s had a considerable impact on the subsequent discourse in Europe and North America.

---

18   Somers, D. (2016). 'Venturi's Discipline' in: De Caigny, S. et al. (eds.). *Autonomous Architecture in Flanders*, p. 189.

19   Ibid.

20   Aureli, P. V. (2013). *The Project of Autonomy: Politics and Architecture within and against Capitalism*. New York: The Temple Hoyne Buell Center for the Study of American Architecture, p. 12.

21   Aureli, P. V. (2013). *The Project of Autonomy*, p. 13.

In their intellectual production, several strains of thought were peculiarly flattened—to some extent, in their association with postmodern architecture—into a theoretical hybrid with its own autonomy. This circulating theory served the emergence of a design method of potential quasi-universal applicability, in Switzerland, Germany, Britain, Spain and, more recently, Belgium. The approach was closely informed by the methodology of *tendenza* (the four-fold engagement with the city, history, typology and form), but also by the impact of Venturi and Scott-Brown, particularly their incursions into the ordinary and the suburban, extracting formal motifs from the language of consumerism. Despite its common sources, the success of this theoretical model can be explained by its capacity to articulate different attitudes and formal productions, based on processes of cultural adaptation and interpretation specific to each location.

Representative of the generation of Northern Swiss (German Swiss) architects most directly influenced by Rossi's teaching, Zurich practitioner Marcel Meili defined the work of his contemporaries by its preoccupation with 'the process of sedimentation of meanings into forms, resulting from the incessant repetition of everyday use'. He held that 'an architecture that could embody more general significations … could be realized through a focus of design on the problem of form … (that) our incursions in the world of the ordinary and the everyday represented a search for collective meanings'.[22] This formulation points once again to a position independent of a regional index and yet associated precisely with cultural formations occurring over the last 30-odd years in specific architectural clusters in Britain, Austria, Germany, Belgium. A similar appeal to ordinary forms and practices as a basis for a common intelligibility comes up in statements about contemporary architecture in Flanders and Brussels. British architect Tony Fretton remarked upon 'the productive relation of these architects with their country, region, city and locale … the development of Flemish cultural and intellectual character as a whole'.[23]

[22] Meili, M. (1991). 'Ein paar Bauten, viele Pläne' in: Disch, P. (ed.). *Architektur in der Deutschen Schweiz*. Lugano: ADV, p. 22.

[23] Fretton, T. (2016). 'The Architects Viewed from a Nearby Island' in: De Caigny, S. et al. (eds.). *Autonomous Architecture in Flanders*, p. 210.

Critic Véronique Patteeuw identified the 'design attitude' in Flanders and Brussels as an architecture at 'eye level'—a sensitivity to the existing manifested through a sense of 'minimal, strategic intervention', and grounded in 'faith in architecture's capacity to create a city'.[24] In dialogue with Maarten Van Den Driessche, Somers also singled out the strategy of mimesis as a way to 'relate [design] to the existing cultural landscape'.[25] For critic Bart Verschaffel, Bovenbouw's design methodology was essentially a response to the Flemish condition of diffuse urban sprawl:

> Bovenbouw's architecture addresses this condition by selecting and collecting elements from this confused and messy environment and condensing them intelligently, thereby augmenting the intensity … they work and play with existing, familiar typologies and building elements, they tolerate and even look for ambiguity, layering, allusions, double meanings. The result is a lucid architecture, one that is not aggressively confrontational but intriguing and stimulating.[26]

The common points of these disparate statements outline a shared referential and methodological horizon. At the same time, they indicate a multitude of thinkers and practitioners in dialogue, equally preoccupied with the analysis and justification of their formal productions on cultural grounds. Similarly, the discourse of various historical and current *tendenze* in Europe can be visualized as regional, nodal points in a web of communities of practice. Their existence depends on what David Schön called 'the reflective practitioner', one who 'shifts from embracing freedom of choice to acceptance of implications, from involvement in the local units to a distanced consideration of the resulting whole, and from a stance of tentative exploration, to one of commitment'.[27] Incidentally, this position is not what one would call autonomous, but specific and socially engaged, pointing to the paradoxal

---

24   Patteeuw, V. (2018). 'How Exportable Is Architecture?' in: *Flanders Architectural Review 13: This is a Mustard Factory*. Antwerp: VAi, p. 250.

25   Somers, D. and Van Den Driessche, M. (2019). 'A Conversation Between Friends', pp. 145–202, p. 173.

26   Verschaffel, B. (2019). 'Agile Thinking' in: Somers, D., Van Den Driessche, M. and Verschaffel, B. *Bovenbouw Architectuur*, p. 17.

27   Schön, D. A. (2017). 'Design as a Reflective Conversation with the Situation' in: Schön, D. A. *The Reflective Practitioner*. London: Routledge, pp. 76–104, p. 102.

use of this notion in the architectural discourse. The reflective practitioner's work oscillates between universal and locally specific constructions of meaning: as a 'global experiment, [it] is also a reflective conversation with the situation'.[28]

Situating the *tendens* in Flanders

The historiography of the various *tendenze* sketched here displays a general, if somewhat misleading, theoretical bias. Architecture's engagement with host cultures and environments has mostly been addressed at a conceptual level—through the emphasis on abstract notions such as typologies, historical references, meanings and signs.

Common patterns emerge in these genealogies of local discourses: stages in which the design method is first formulated by a cluster of critical practices, then consolidated and generalized as a modus operandi among their peers; the dialogues of reflective practitioners and critics in publications and group exhibitions; the formation of professional cultures under the influence of charismatic figures such as Rossi, Venturi, Kolhoff, Meili and many others, which leads to the transfer of related methods between cultural contexts and between architectural generations. In the context of the Low Countries, Christian Kieckens is often mentioned as the influential teacher-practitioner who introduced a generation of Belgian and Dutch students to a series of later *tendenze*—in Switzerland, Britain, etc.—which provided a more direct model for the new architecture in Flanders and Brussels, as a new *tendens* in itself.

However, the fascination with the theoretical implications of autonomy runs the risk of overlooking the powerful impact of political and pragmatic considerations on the professional culture of these regional clusters.[29]

---

28   Schön, D. A. (2017). 'Design as a Reflective Conversation with the Situation', p. 103.

29   To give a historical example: even before the Italians were done theorizing *La Tendenza*, buildings designed according to their principles were being constructed in neighbouring Ticino. The quality and critical mass of this built production claimed the sphere of influence from Italian architecture, highlighting the peculiar misalignment of cultural and national boundaries in Lombardy (which Ticino had, historically, been part of). The Ticinese swiftness in assimilating the theoretical foci of the Italians was a matter of political conjecture. The cantonal policy of educational reform in the late 1960s and 1970s allowed the construction of the schools, gymnasia and kindergartens with which the young Ticinese architects started their professional careers. Additionally, it was the momentous decision of liberal-minded officials that led to public competitions and commissions, without which the 'new architecture in Ticino' would never have happened.

The characterization of a tentative *tendens* in Flanders and Brussels—as well as related phenomena in the last four decades in Switzerland, Britain, Germany, etc.—must be considered in connection to its immediate historical, professional and political landscape. Specifically, this recent blossoming is directly connected to the authority of two professional institutions: the position of *Bouwmeester* (Government Architect), established in 1999, and the architectural competition system, which it directly enabled. In the last 20 years, almost 700 open call competitions were initiated in Flanders and Brussels, a quarter of which were commissioned by the government and almost half by local authorities.[30] This impressive number of entry points to prestigious commissions has served the creation of a public architecture of high quality. While the political framework imposes no a priori stipulation of stylistic or conceptual terms, it stimulates the discussion of fundamental questions, at both the architectural and political level. It creates a sense of responsibility, shared by commissioning bodies and commissioned architects, as regards the role of architecture in the built environment and in culture. The recent exhibition *Open Call. 20 Years of Publicly Commissioned Architecture*, celebrating the competition system and the position of Government Architect, pertinently summarized this discussion:

> A recurrent issue is how a building today can convey its public character and its specific function. Which architecture is appropriate for which type of institution? Should an administrative centre radiate transparency and efficiency, or informality, perhaps even domesticity? A crematorium must be dignified, but how much symbolism and what type of symbolism do we want here? And how can architecture give shape to these values?[31]

---

30 Liefooghe, M. and Van Den Driessche, M. (2019). *Open Call. 20 Years of Publicly Commissioned Architecture*. Brussels: Team Vlaams Bouwmeester, p. 5.

31 Liefooghe, M. and Van Den Driessche, M. (2019). *Open Call*, p. 27.

The commissioning system emphasizes the societal values of architecture: its contribution to urban renewal, the question of collective intelligibility as one of 'arresting and appropriate performance'.[32] Architecture's sense of integrity is fostered and articulated also at a professional level. The transparency of the process engenders what seems—from the outside, certainly—a healthy architectural dialogue. It also offers genuine opportunities for new talent to emerge.

In parallel, the local architectural culture is shored up by educational institutions that foster precisely the kind of professional discourse that creates architectural networks and sustains the quality of their production. It is no coincidence that the Generation '74 was named after the year of graduation from the school of architecture in Ghent, a significant basin for theoretical and architectural knowledge (much as the great majority of the Ticinese 'Young Turks' so-called had graduated from ETH Zurich, where many returned to teach). The combined resources of KU Leuven (with its multiple campuses unifying various architectural cultures), Ghent University, Hasselt University and the University of Antwerp have created a powerful architectural ecology of practitioners, writers and educators, many of whom operate in parallel activities in practice and academia. Nowhere is this professional discourse more consistently articulated than in the exhibitions and publications of the Flanders Architecture Institute (VAi), founded in 2001, whose yearbooks have become a vehicle for its wider dissemination.[33] With the risk of idealizing the situation on the ground, it is important to situate the built production gathered in this installation in all the theatres of its operation: institutional and informal, pragmatic and abstract, theoretical and pragmatic. This is what the 'composite presence' of Bovenbouw's Venice installation points to: a shared culture of architecture as a surrogate for the irretrievable unity of the city.

---

32   Somers, D. and Van Den Driessche, M. (2019). 'A Conversation Between Friends', pp. 145–202, p. 173.

33   The yearbooks preceded the formation of the VAi, being published between 1990 and 2009, initially as a government publication, under the title *Jaarboek architectuur Vlaanderen = Yearbook architecture Flanders = Annuaire architecture Flandre*. Since 2012, five biennial thematic issues of the *Flanders Architectural Review* have been published: *Radical Commonplaces* (no. 10 / 2012), *Embedded Architectures* (no. 11 / 2014), *Tailored Architecture* (no. 12 / 2016), *This is a Mustard Factory* (no. 13 / 2018) and *When Attitudes Take Form* (no. 14 / 2020).

Projects

44 **Observation tower** Baeten Hylebos Architecten
46 **Zoersel House** Arjaan De Feyter Interior Architects
48 **Masonry House** Schenk Hattori Architecture Atelier
50 **Silos—Kanaal** Stéphane Beel Architects
52 **Studio SDS** GRAUX & BAEYENS architecten
54 **Youth Centre 'De Lichting'** Raamwerk
56 **Chapel of Our Lady of the Muizenhoek** PULS architecten
58 **Montigny live-work units** META architectuurbureau
60 **Werfstraat** Bovenbouw Architectuur
62 **Zegel** Hub
64 **House VDB** Collectief Noord Architecten
66 **Kioskplaats Police Station** De Smet Vermeulen architecten
68 **Office and apartment Bailleul** Marie-José Van Hee architecten
70 **Community Centre De Steen** ono architectuur
72 **BLAF t1G** BLAF Architecten
74 **One Room Hotel** dmvA
76 **House L-C** GRAUX & BAEYENS architecten
78 **The Majin House, care home** Raamwerk and Van Gelder Tilleman Architecten
80 **VDB social housing** VERS.A
82 **Lalo** murmuur architecten
84 **Van Artevelde apartments** BULK architecten
86 **Apostelhuizen Studio** De Smet Vermeulen architecten
88 **Apart huis arts** architecten de vylder vinck taillieu
90 **Youth Centre 'Jeunes'** AgwA in collaboration with Ferrière Architectes
92 **Maarschalk Gerardstraat 5** Eagles of Architecture
94 **The Little Prince** Dhooge & Meganck Architectuur
96 **House Verbrande Brug** architecten de vylder vinck taillieu
in collaboration with Doorzon interieurarchitecten

Louis De Mey and Dirk Somers

- 98 RLN, rehabilitation centre ^{URA Yves Malysse Kiki Verbeeck}
- 100 OFFICE 229: Public Library ^{OFFICE Kersten Geers David Van Severen}
- 102 Organ loft for the Contius organ, St Michael's Church ^{360 Architecten}
- 104 State Archives Ghent ^{Robbrecht en Daem architecten in collaboration with Arch & Teco}
- 106 Walled house with winter garden ^{STUDIOLO architectuur in collaboration with Koen Matthys}
- 108 Olijftakstraat ^{FELT architecture & design}
- 110 Dambruggestraat ^{Dierendonckblancke architecten}
- 112 Twaalfkameren ^{Dierendonckblancke architecten}
- 114 Double house Kattenberg ^{Architecten Broekx-Schiepers}
- 116 Wolters House ^{tim peeters architecten}
- 118 Prins Leopold ^{ono architectuur}
- 120 Meir corner building ^{DMT architecten}
- 122 Langemark-Poelkapelle town hall extension ^{Tom Thys architecten}
- 124 De Nor ^{FVWW architecten in collaboration with Dennis Tyfus}
- 126 Media Building ^{Robbrecht en Daem architecten & Dierendonckblancke architecten in collaboration with VK Engineering & Arup}
- 128 Elementary School Zarren ^{FELT architecture & design}
- 130 Schaerdeke social housing ^{Architectenbureau Bart Dehaene in collaboration with artist Dirk Zoete}
- 132 DC-V house and office ^{Vermeiren—De Coster Architecten}
- 134 Verzoeningstraat ^{Poot Architectuur}
- 136 Broek ^{Tim Rogge Architectuur Studio}
- 138 Soubry ^{Coussée & Goris architecten}
- 140 Service building container park ^{ectv architecten Els Claessens en Tania Vandenbussche}
- 142 Ryhove Urban Factory ^{Trans architectuur stedenbouw}

Baeten Hylebos Architecten
Observation tower

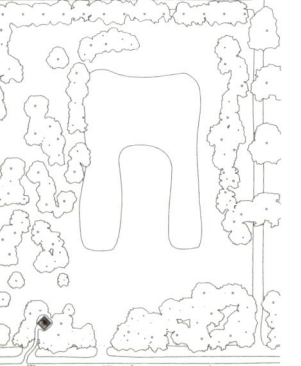

In the midst of one of Flanders' scarce nature areas, the Boudelo Foundation, a small landmark has been erected to overlook the surroundings. Made entirely out of wood, the observation tower was designed in a very simple and lucid manner by Baeten Hylebos Architecten. The tower consists of a square, two-storey spiralling staircase inside a wooden framework. Painted in a modest dark-green, the construction has been clad in wooden planks on the inside, letting the constructive elements determine its appearance. Outlook openings disrupt this tectonic system and prevent the façade from looking rigid. The landmark function of the tower is a territorial act, one that 'reclaims' the natural area. It revisits it, makes it accessible, opens it up to the public. Paradoxically, we need architecture to make us aware of the few remaining natural reserves. We also need it as a political act to prevent it from being developed.

Arjaan De Feyter Interior Architects
Zoersel House

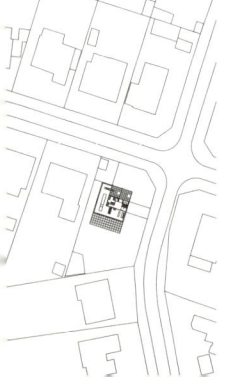

Conceived in 1969 in the spirit of radical modernism, this square, two-storey villa was recently renovated by Arjaan De Feyter Interior Architects. While one might suspect the villa of being situated within a wide landscape, it is positioned on a corner parcel in a generic Flemish allotment that is attached to the ribbon development between Antwerp and Turnhout. Contrasting with the farmhouse-style brick houses surrounding it, the villa is constructed as a steel skeleton in a perfect, nine-square grid. The villa shows itself as a layered object, at once exposing its structure and being selectively transparent through the use of transparent and opaque glass infills. The generic structure marks out the house as an outsider in this neighbourhood, precisely because it introduces this universalist modernist idiom into the very mundane and dreary reality of the surroundings.

Schenk Hattori Architecture Atelier
Masonry House

Schenk Hattori Architecture Atelier extended this quite mundane house with a new entrance hall. The existing house was also wrapped in an insulating coat. Beside the entrance, the new brick skin moves away from the former façade. The gap between the two façades becomes a new staircase, making it possible for one of the upstairs rooms to function autonomously from the rest of the upper floor. The architectural idiom of the additions is serene and seeks harmony with the existing house. The residence was given new layers that add depth and complexity to its retro farmhouse style.

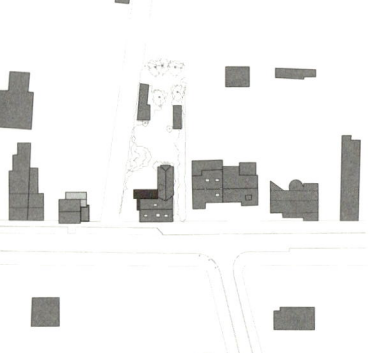

49

Stéphane Beel Architects
Silos—Kanaal

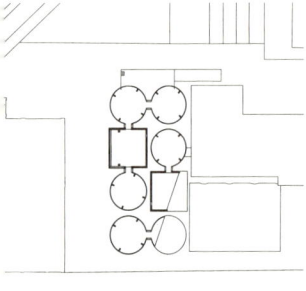

Stéphane Beel Architects was asked to contribute to the large residential development of a nineteenth-century industrial site along a canal. The architects approached the liquor distillery prudently. A group of eight silos was preserved as a figure in the landscape, the main liquor house being replaced by a white residential tower of the same height. Minimal incisions were made in the silos to ensure their solidity. Two of the silos were replaced by square towers that bridge the architectural language of the austere silos and the more open character of the adjacent, newly constructed residential tower. This operation offers fully glazed living rooms to the apartments, while still preserving the *Gestalt* of the industrial landmark.

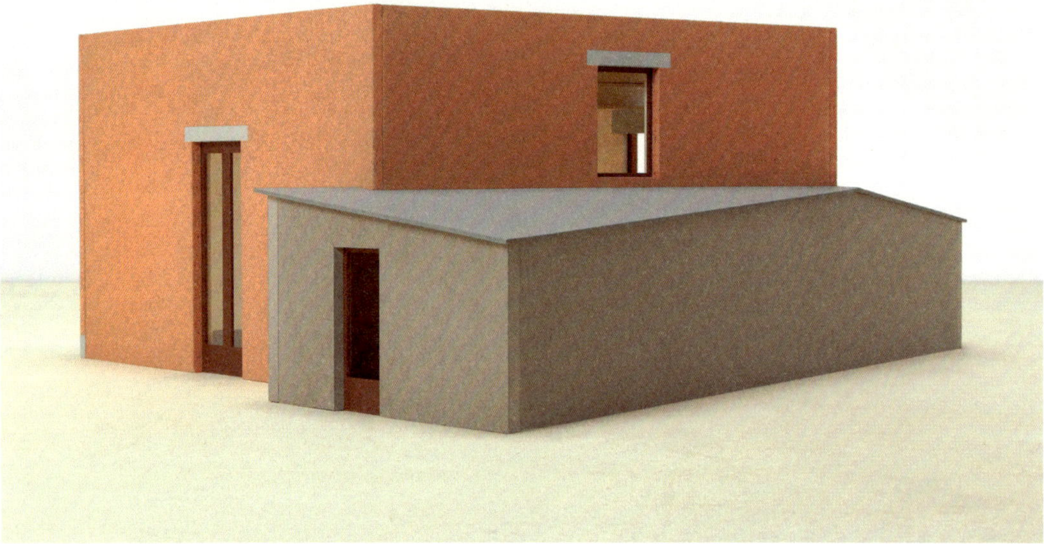

GRAUX & BAEYENS architecten
Studio SDS

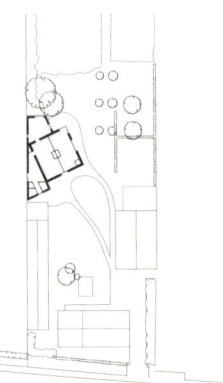

In a rural area of Flanders, GRAUX & BAEYENS architecten designed an extension to a typical farm as an atelier and artist studio. The studio is an annex in grey concrete blocks, reminiscent of the self-built extensions so typical of Flanders. Although attached to the complex of small volumes, the atelier was conceived as an autonomous form in the landscape. The compact, box-shaped volume is accentuated with crisp concrete lintels and vertically exaggerated doorways. Its light-red brick façade appears fresh among grey concrete blocks and the farm's rusty-red brick volumes. The low concrete plinth around the volume was pulled into the interior, where it became a bench. The concrete lintels equally determine the atmosphere of the interior space, contrasting with the whitewashed brick walls.

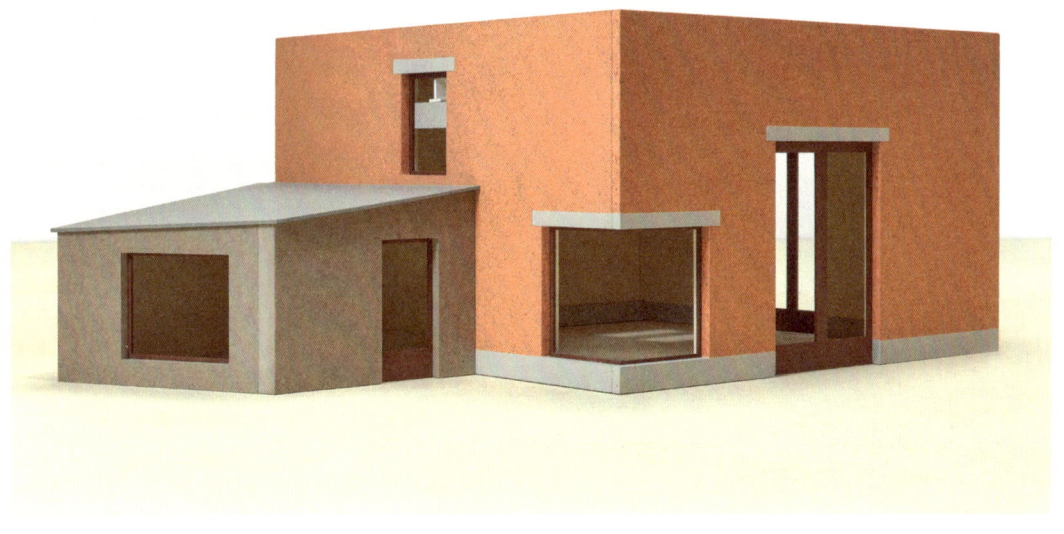

Raamwerk
Youth Centre 'De Lichting'

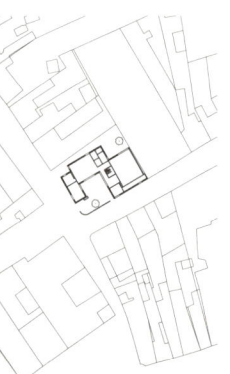

In the rural village of Lichtervelde, Raamwerk delivered a new youth centre through the Winvorm competition procedure. The composition of simple rectangular volumes in a most common red brick stands out in this context through its radical simplicity and modest contextuality. By breaking up the volume into a composition of smaller entities, the building enters into a conversation with the surrounding village fabric. Moreover, the red brick connects the youth centre with the building block and its similarly coloured façades and roofs. The humble building materials are elevated by different brick sizes and sharp window frames and gates in matching tones. While the facility feels very familiar in its appearance and scale, these delicate shifts turn the building into a bright exception in its generic environment.

55

PULS architecten
Chapel of Our Lady of the Muizenhoek

A seemingly forgotten chapel on the side of a road was given a radical update by PULS architecten. The existing trees surrounding the chapel already suggested the nave of a church. The architects therefore emphasized this gesture by completing the cluster of column-like trunks with the missing point in the configuration. To further underline this gesture, the architects created a tiny enclosed garden—a reference to the medieval *hortus conclusus*—by means of the floor treatment and two benches. The white steel benches are abstract renditions of majestic church benches with a very high backrest. The chapel itself was given a new gate, a modest contemporary interpretation of the baroque language of the chapel.

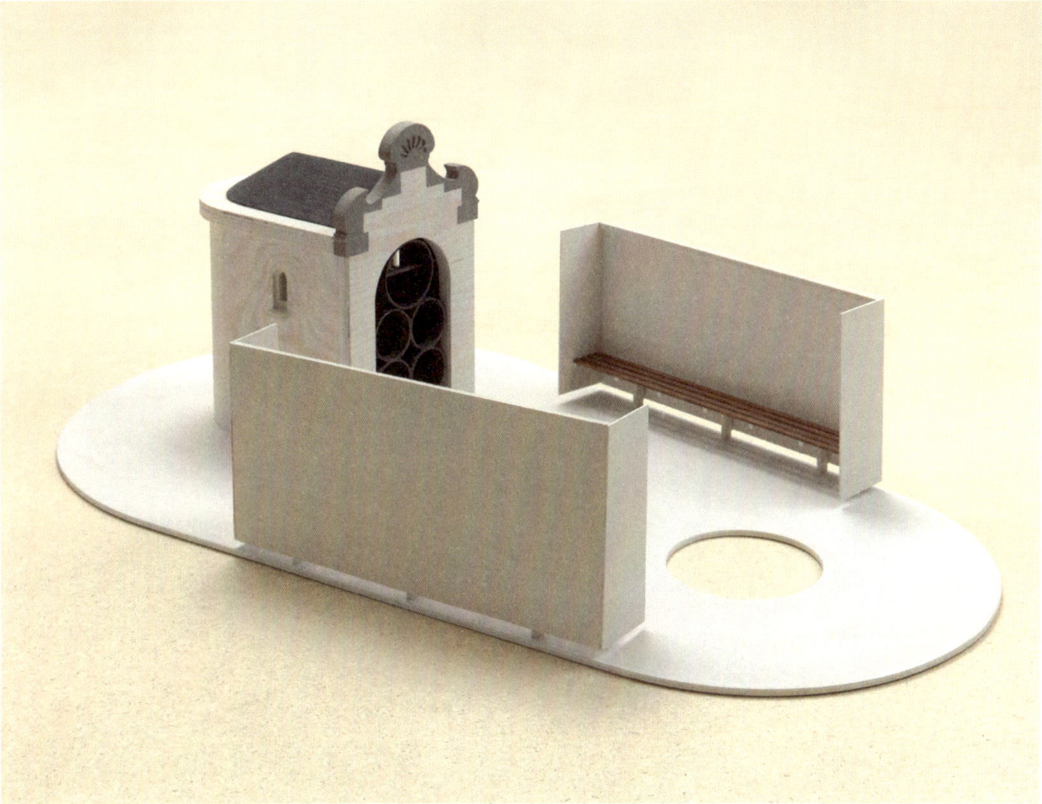

META architectuurbureau
Montigny live-work units

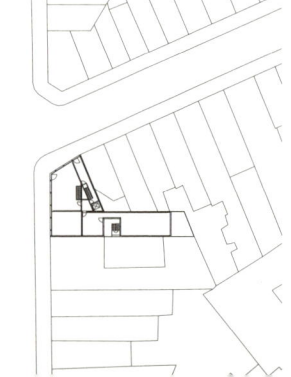

META architectuurbureau is behind this mixed-use building that houses apartments, offices and, on the ground level, a piano shop. The building was designed as an 'intelligent ruin' with an open plan in which office spaces as well as apartments can be housed. The circulation core was positioned at the back so as to maximize the enjoyment of daylight. The white, prefabricated concrete façades were conceived as a tectonic stacking of floor plates and columns. The windows behind one of the two façades were pulled back to create an intermediate zone for terraces. The recesses of the façade create an expressive shadow play that adds life to the barefaced carcass.

60

Bovenbouw architectuur
Werfstraat

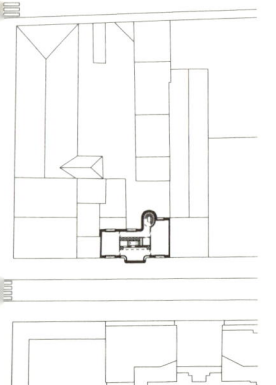

In designing this residential building in the centre of Brussels, Bovenbouw architectuur drew inspiration from the city's rich tradition of town houses. The façade is dominated by the abstract figure of a blind bay that simultaneously marks the entrance and structures the façade composition. The blind bay provides interesting oblique views into the narrow street and supports a terrace on the living-room floor. Although somewhat industrial in appearance, the elevations are conceived in intricate undulating brickwork, not unfamiliar to the sculptural treatment of art nouveau façades around the city. A complementary undulating treatment marks the route from the front door to the stairs leading upwards.

Hub
Zegel

On a corner of one of Antwerp's major access roads to the city centre, Hub designed a serene mixed-use building that houses residences, offices for the district police and an entrance to a metro station. It is composed of a three-storey plinth and a three-storey tower set back from the corner. The plinth completes the existing street profile, while the tower marks the corner and engages in a dialogue with the apartment building on the opposite corner. The façade was conceived as a generic rhythm of bays, with shallowly recessed windows. While the rhythm acts as a mask covering the different programmes behind it, the windows nonetheless underline the difference. The upper floors that house the residential programme have portrait windows, while the office floors below have larger bays with square windows. The tectonics of the façade have been accentuated by the corner windows of the plinth and the 'open' corner solution of the tower.

Collectief Noord Architecten
House VDB

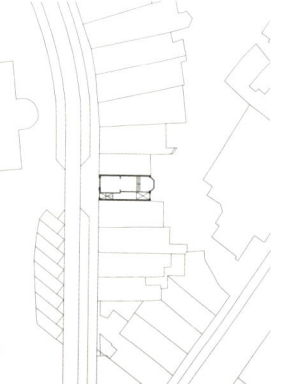

This historical terraced house in Antwerp was renovated by Collectief Noord Architecten. The rear of the house was raised slightly to create a split-level system with visual relations between one floor and another. At the back, the existing bay window on the first floor was extended downwards to the level of the garden. The bay window lets daylight penetrate deep into the half-sunken kitchen space. This way, the formerly dark basement has been turned into a bright space to cook, eat and live. Moreover, through the open stairs in the heart of the house, the bay window reinforces the visual link between the kitchen space and the first floor. Outside, the figure of the bay was treated very subtly, as if it had always been there. This original, commonplace architectural figure is now slightly distorted and has become a moment of fun.

De Smet Vermeulen architecten
Kioskplaats Police Station

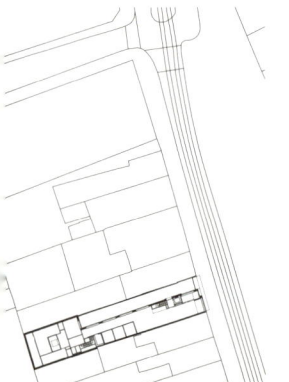

In order to raise the public visibility and lower the threshold of the police station in Hoboken, the building was moved to a central location on an elongated public square. On the deep, narrow parcel, De Smet Vermeulen architecten designed a station that is proportioned as an urban house, without a generic office façade. A higher, set-back volume on top was positioned to the left, seeking connection to the small apartment building. The roof terrace on the right reads in turn as a humble gesture towards the house on the right. The façade in a light-blue glazed brick was conceived as a public moment in the street, with a clock and a canopy to open it up to the street. The gate and front door of the demolished house were recuperated and add a commonplace historical dimension to the façade of the building.

67

Marie-José Van Hee architecten
Office and apartment Bailleul

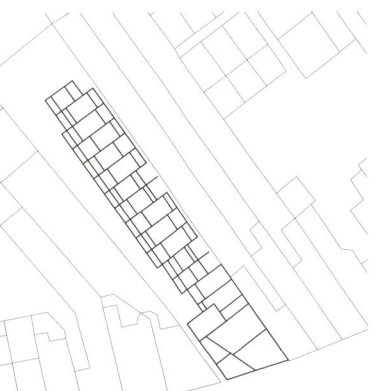

On a very deep plot near Ghent's main train station, Marie-José Van Hee architecten designed a house combined with office spaces. The living quarters are located on the street side, starting from the first floor. The workspaces occupy the garden in the form of a glass pavilion, on top of a basement archive. The archive was conceived as a concrete basin that at some point could be turned into a pond while the steel structure of the office space could become a pergola overgrown with greenery. The shallow green margins that surround the office pavilion and the slight deviations in the modular system create a meandering space along the axis of the garden. By contrast, the street façade appears more solid and quieter, with its greyish plaster, three planes of rhythmically subdivided windows, and natural-stone plinth.

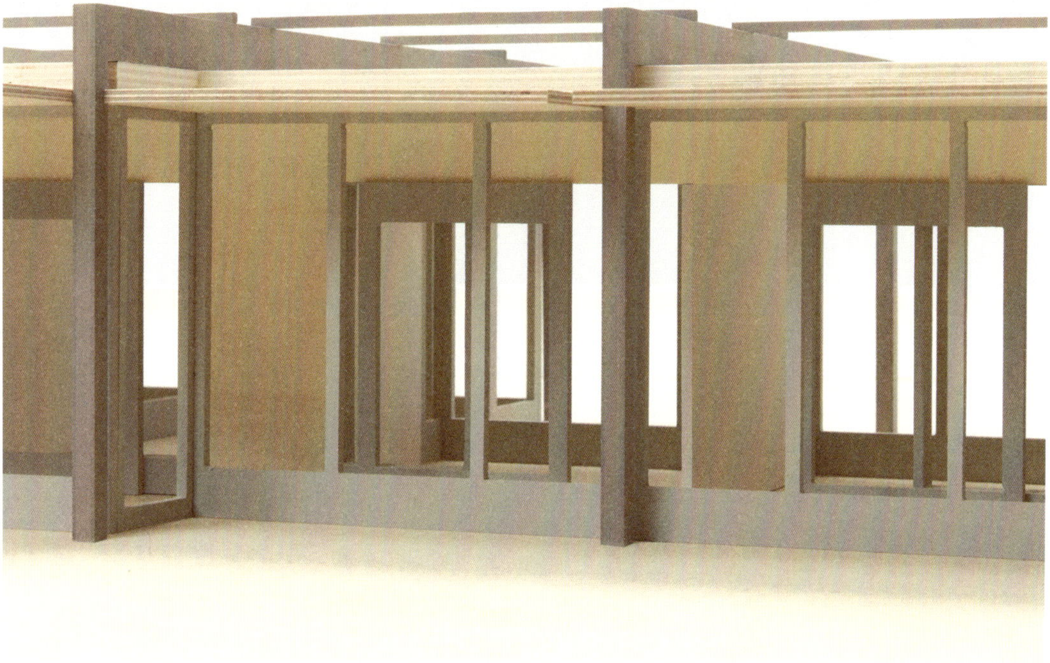

ono architectuur
Community Centre De Steen

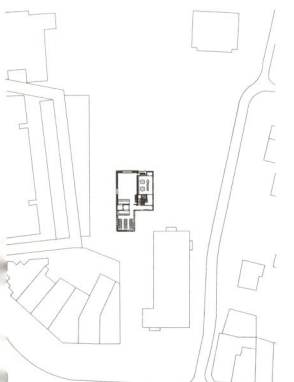

In the heart of the village of Bocholt, in the province of Limburg, a community centre was erected on a rather indeterminate terrain closed off from the main street. Ono architectuur established a contemporary monumental gesture with a solid volume that organizes its surroundings from this setback position. On the ground floor, the compact, cube-like volume has an annex that contains a bar giving onto the square. The staircase and technical facilities stand out on top of the building and provide access to the roof terrace. The façades are structured in a rather classical way, with a regular rhythm of large vertical windows that emphasize the centre's modest monumentality.

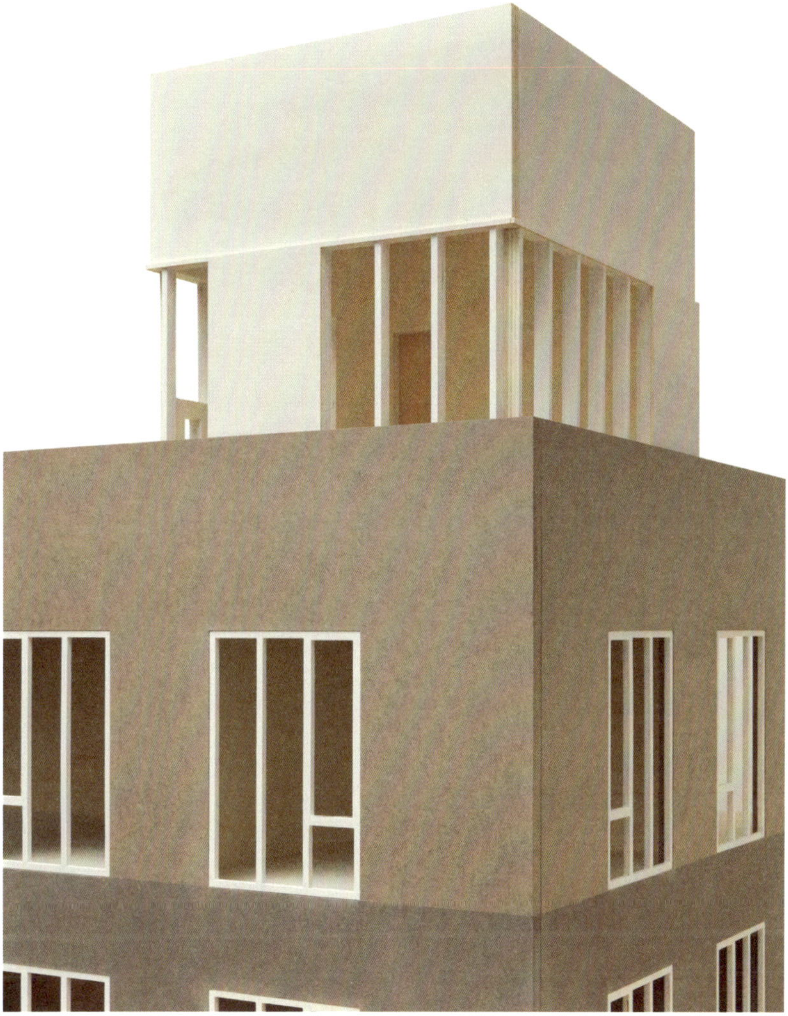

BLAF Architecten
BLAF tlG

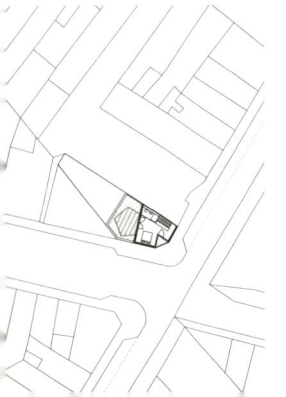

For the roof extension of this corner house in the city of Ghent, BLAF Architecten opted for a sober monochrome volume. From the street, the extension looks like two connected rooms on top; in plan it appears to be an L-shaped volume. The volume was placed on a bold roof edge, making the extension seem like a 'hat' for the existing building. This crisp 'head covering' functions as an inverted plinth for the existing building. The plain grey plaster contrasts starkly with the weathered brick façades, and the fine zinc roof edges counter the dark wooden window frames below. Without altering the original house, the appearance of the building has been updated and refreshed, and the street corner has become a characteristic moment in the streetscape.

dmvA
One Room Hotel

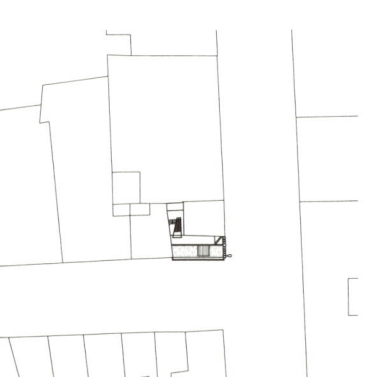

Heritage requirements combine with the new logics of tourism in this tiny medieval house. On an incredibly narrow L-shaped plot in the centre of Antwerp, dmvA designed a 'one room hotel' for a private investor. The three floors of the sixteenth-century house are connected spatially by means of stairs and voids. These spatial links are reinforced by the creation of a bright atmosphere with a white-washed interior space. Mirrors enlarge the narrow spaces and offer unexpected views. The generous amount of circulation space results in an architectural parcours that leads up to two tiny roof terraces overlooking the city.

75

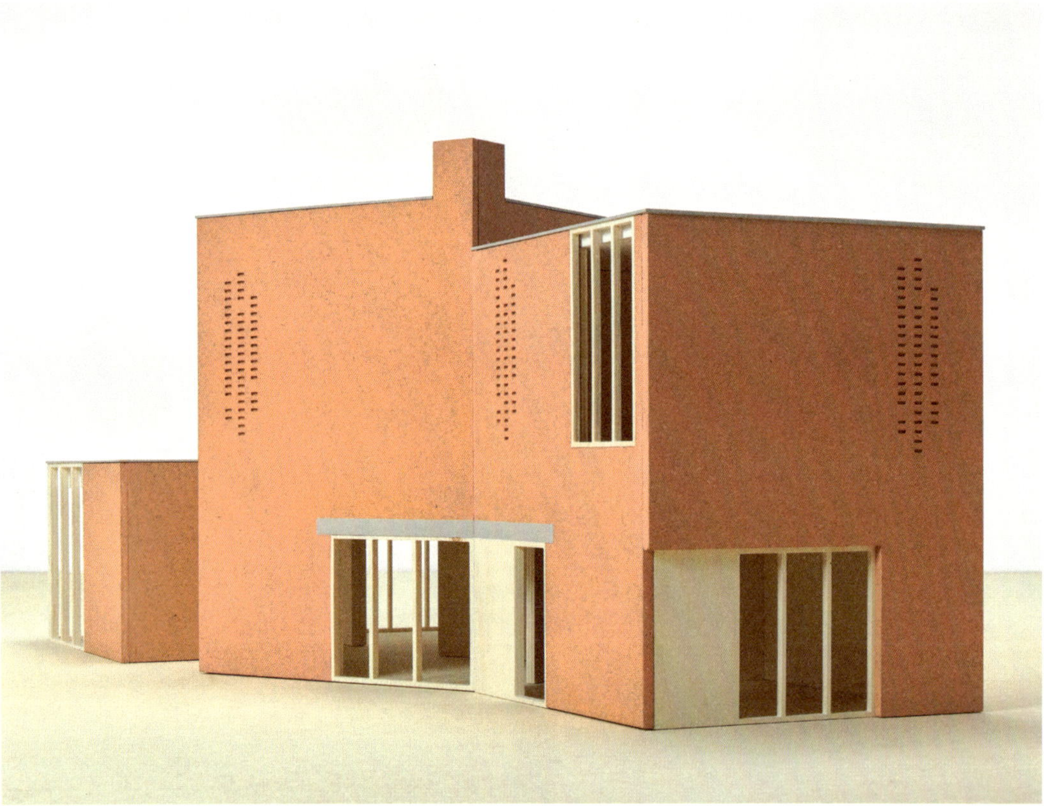

GRAUX & BAEYENS architecten
House L-C

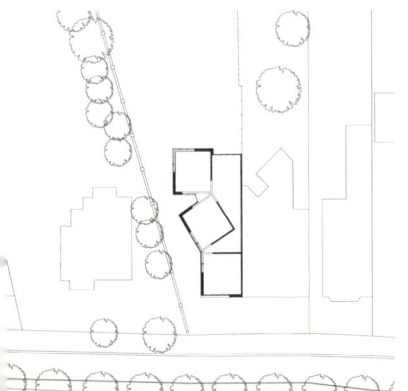

The semi-terraced house GRAUX & BAEYENS architecten designed for a tapering building plot is composed as a series of three connected volumes of different heights. Each has an equal square footprint and the middle one has been rotated. A staircase nestles in the wedge between the two first volumes. The points of connection between the three parts were conceived as complex concrete knots. These not only make up sturdy lintels in the façade composition, but are also exposed on the interior and make these rotation junctions explicitly present in the interior. The lintels were combined with rustic brickwork in the façades and adorned with decorative openwork that lets light into a dressing room.

Raamwerk and Van Gelder Tilleman Architecten
The Majin House, care home

Near one of Ghent's beguinages, Raamwerk and Van Gelder Tilleman Architecten designed a care home for cancer patients and their loved ones. The project comprised the renovation of a town house and a new corner building attached to it. The renovated building and the new volume are spatially connected through a patio-like garden. The new façade was conceived as a stacking of similar concrete panels, each panel more or less square-shaped and punctured by a large window at the bottom centre. On the corner, the panels are stacked with alternating structural overlaps, suggesting the structural bond between the panels.

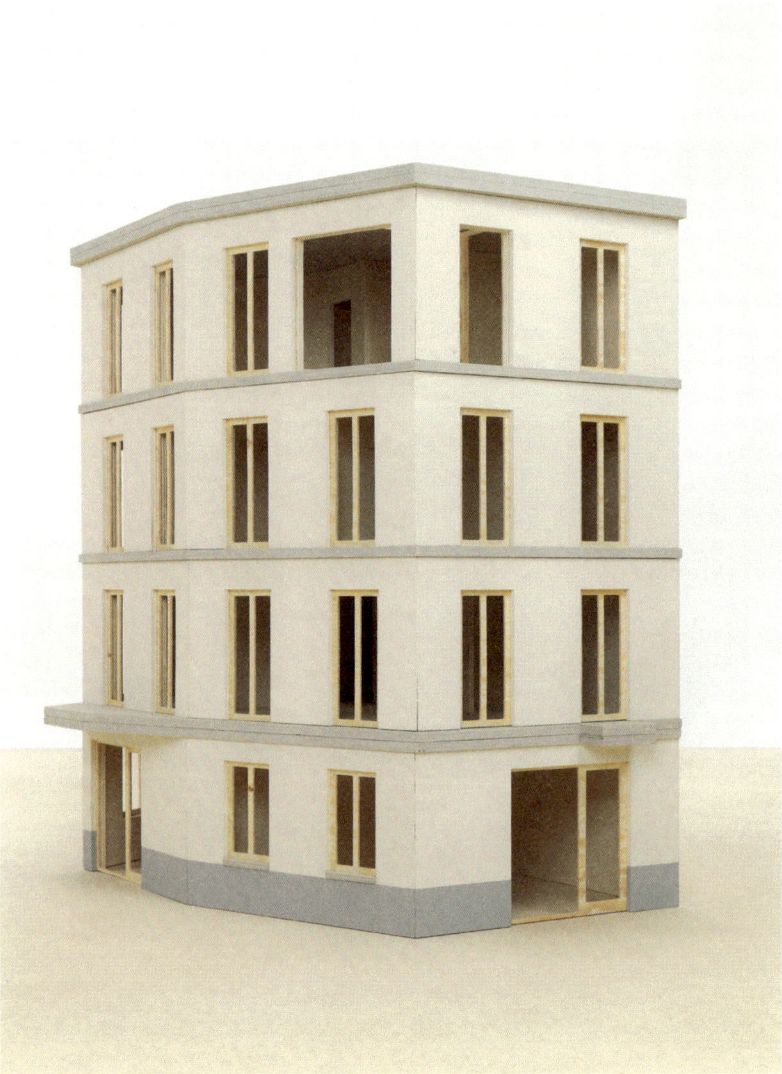

VERS.A
VDB social housing

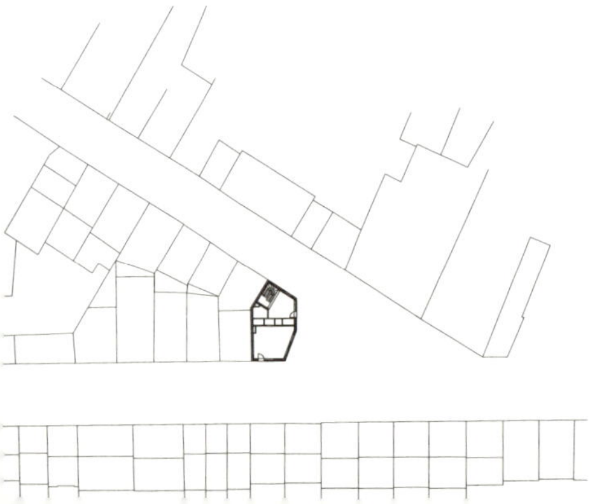

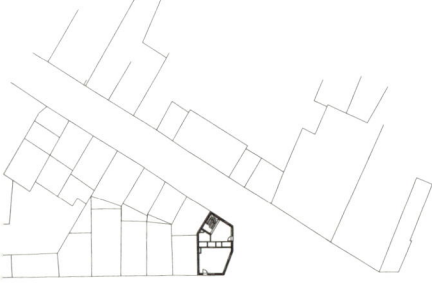

VERS.A constructed this rhythmic residential building on the corner of a block in the municipality of Ixelles in Brussels. The narrow plot offered no outdoor space. As a result, the white façades are characterized by a lot of windows that are distributed rhythmically. The windows rest on horizontal concrete lintels that run along the façade at the level of each of the floor slabs. As a variation on this façade structure, the ground floor has a plinth in blue stone on which the windows gently sit. The cornice in turn picks up the trope of the lintels in an exaggerated way. The building seems like a bent Italian palazzo: firm but gracious, and generous to the public.

murmuur architecten
Lalo

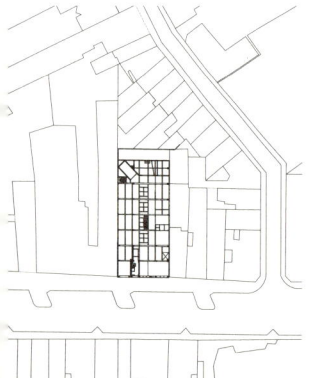

A former apartment building was renovated by murmuur architecten and extended with two residential storeys. On the ground floor, the concrete structure was purified and opened up to house the current bike shop. The two additional storeys on top grant the building a height that accords better with the façade's length. The top floor has been clad in grey planks that contrast with the light façade and seems like a hat placed on top of the building. While the renovation and extension were carefully accorded with the existing proportions and idiom of the façade, the architects underlined the building's dignity, making it a friend worthy of the surrounding town houses.

BULK architecten
Van Artevelde apartments

BULK architecten was commissioned to design a small apartment building on a long but narrow corner plot. The stacked apartments consist of a simple enfilade of spaces along the façade. This enfilade has been expressed in the façade, which is constructed out of sand-coloured brickwork. The interior rooms are visible in planes of slightly recessed brickwork that anchor the respective windows. The shop on the ground floor is marked by the plinth in brighter vanilla bricks. The volume of this explicitly urban building was raised at the corner. By leaving out a window at the top of the shorter elevation, the building gains a strong presence on the square.

De Smet Vermeulen architecten
Apostelhuizen Studio

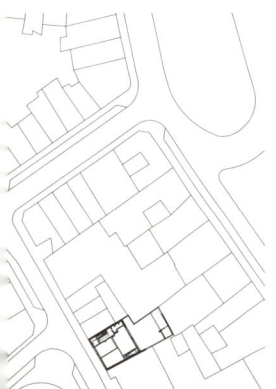

This studio house in the centre of Ghent was designed by De Smet Vermeulen architecten, who are currently using it as their office. The front façade is very welcoming. Its large windows show a room on the ground floor, stairs passing in front of the glass on the completely transparent first floor, and a hint of a room on the top floor. This open façade was conceived as a self-supporting skin in front of the building and composed in a highly tectonic manner. Two wide concrete beams with visible plank shuttering mark the different storeys. They are supported by expressive brickwork and steel profiles. Voids behind the façade emphasize the structure and draw light deep into the house.

architecten de vylder vinck taillieu
apart huis arts

Three terraced houses were positioned on top of a medical office in this design by architecten de vylder vinck taillieu. The office was extended into the garden by means of a low volume with a green roof and three sculptural roof lights. The interior spaces of both the medical office and the residences are designed as a play of structural elements in red industrial brick, concrete bricks, concrete floors and wooden floors. The façade is a continuation of these basic construction materials in a more structured composition that fits the street. On top of the façade, three odd roof dormers appear to rest on the roof edge, with parts of the façade brickwork extending next to or between them. The balconies of the living rooms are sheltered from view by means of open brickwork. The humble materials and their distorted tectonic expressions turn out to be a leitmotif in this take on Flemish terraced housing.

AgwA in collaboration with Ferrière Architectes
Youth Centre 'Jeunes'

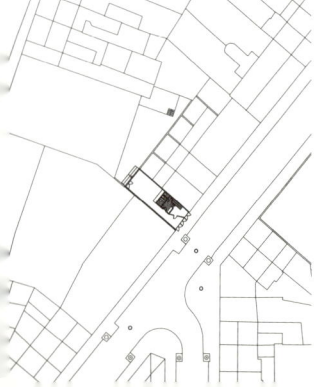

This youth centre in Brussels was designed as a contemporary town house by AgwA. The façade is composed of horizontal strips, alternating precast concrete elements with strips of windows. The windows have been divided into vertical segments by heavy wooden frames that tectonically appear to support the concrete bands. On the inside, the wooden window frames add a subtle luxurious gesture to the sober spaces. The interior was conceived as a split-level system, offering spatial openness while still defining discrete rooms. Designed inside out, the building breathes a straightforward brutalist atmosphere that contributes to the varied streetscape of Brussels.

Eagles of Architecture
Maarschalk Gerardstraat 5

Behind the town house that Eagles of Architecture had already refurbished, a second phase of the project comprised the renovation of the courtyard and the conversion of a building in the back into an office space. In front of the building's neoclassical façade, Eagles of Architecture added a greenhouse glass wall. The wooden beams that make up the ceiling appear to continue on the outside and form a small canopy over the glass wall. Through the glass, a window opening in the former façade is rimmed with light bulbs. This playful frame of lights nods to an articulated window frame in the glass wall and intensifies the dialogue between the classical and the industrial façade.

Dhooge & Meganck Architectuur
The Little Prince

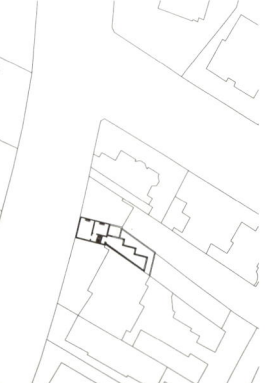

Dhooge & Meganck Architectuur designed this sawtooth extension to a terraced house on a narrow, curved plot. The structure of the new volume was conceived as three remarkably shaped wooden rafters. They start as a column on the ground floor and grow into a chamfered beam that leans onto the party wall. High-up windows draw soft northern light into these living quarters. The form of the rafters was reinterpreted in the design of the metal balustrades for the first-floor windows. The three wooden trusses determine the project in formal, rhythmic and spatial ways. They also create an unexpected and expressive coherence.

**architecten de vylder vinck taillieu
in collaboration with
Doorzon interieurarchitecten**
House Verbrande Brug

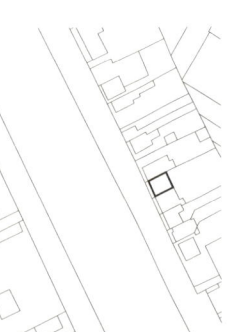

Overlooking the Zenne canal, a garage was converted into a house by architecten de vylder vinck taillieu and Doorzon. The garage's one-storey perimeter wall and its gate were kept in their original state. Within this perimeter, a new volume was added. The main axes of the new volume were rotated to give this terraced house a different relation to the canal. In the triangular interspace between the existing perimeter wall and the new oblique façade, an outdoor antechamber emerges as a welcoming gesture. The living quarters are on the first floor, offering long views over the canal. These large windows resonate with the dimensions of the gate on the ground floor. The gabled roof in common dark tiles finishes the almost classical threefold structure of the front façade.

URA Yves Malysse Kiki Verbeeck
RLN, rehabilitation centre

Behind the renovated façade of this three-storey town house, URA Yves Malysse Kiki Verbeeck inserted a new construction that comprises five levels housing a rehabilitation centre for children. From the street already, one can see hints of the floor plates and a staircase that do not align with the façade openings. One such misalignment of a ceiling that is lower than the front door opening was turned into a welcoming portico. Behind the town house, three pavilions were constructed in the garden that span the whole width of the plot. These divide the long garden into three garden rooms and establish a connection with a street at the back. The whole project can be read as a gradient that subtly mediates the programme from a dynamic road in front up to a quiet street behind.

OFFICE
Kersten Geers David Van Severen
OFFICE 229: Public Library

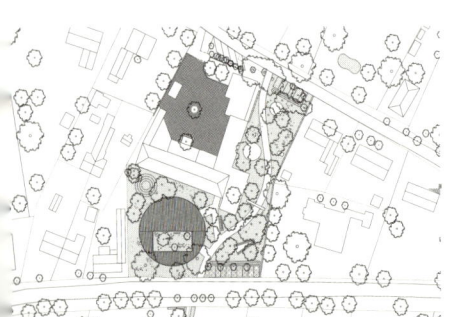

For the Open Call competition for a new library in Sint-Martens-Latem, OFFICE Kersten Geers David Van Severen proposed a simple yet richly nuanced building. The library is perfectly circular in plan, and so has no explicit front or back. Instead, it faces all sides equally. This gesture reinstates the public character of the school building behind it. Surprisingly, the circular building is adorned with a pitched roof. As such, the design merges a very abstract and a highly vernacular gesture into one difficult whole. Inside, a large patio effortlessly organizes the library and reading spaces, and makes the building inward-looking. With a coat of expressive brickwork, a corrugated metal roof and yellow doors, the façade of this almost schematic design will be realized in an equally sharp set of materials that inject a dash of 'pop' in this rural town.

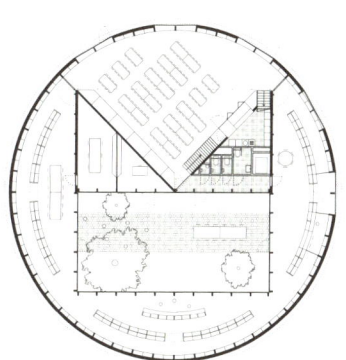

360 architecten
Organ loft for the Contius organ, St Michael's Church

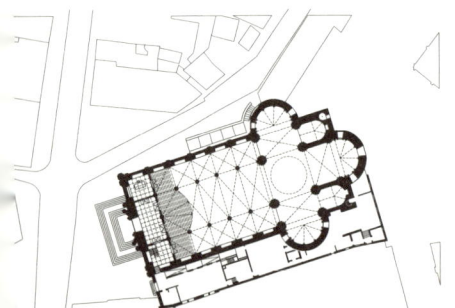

For the design of a new organ loft in the narthex of St Michael's Church in Leuven, 360 architecten adopted a restrained stance, but without hiding the intervention. The structure of the organ's balcony was kept simple, resting on two heavy columns that mark the central corridor of the nave, subtly forcing churchgoers to select a route as they enter the church. The structural beams were kept visible from below in a pattern radiating away from one of the interior façade's pillars. The balcony is protected by a delicate balustrade that folds itself around the balcony and behind two columns of the church. The balustrade was designed as a contemporary answer to the surrounding interior. The wooden panels were punched with a regular and repetitive ajour pattern. Looking for an appropriate contemporaneity, the architects designed a frivolous and complex figure, mimicking the baroque decorations of the church.

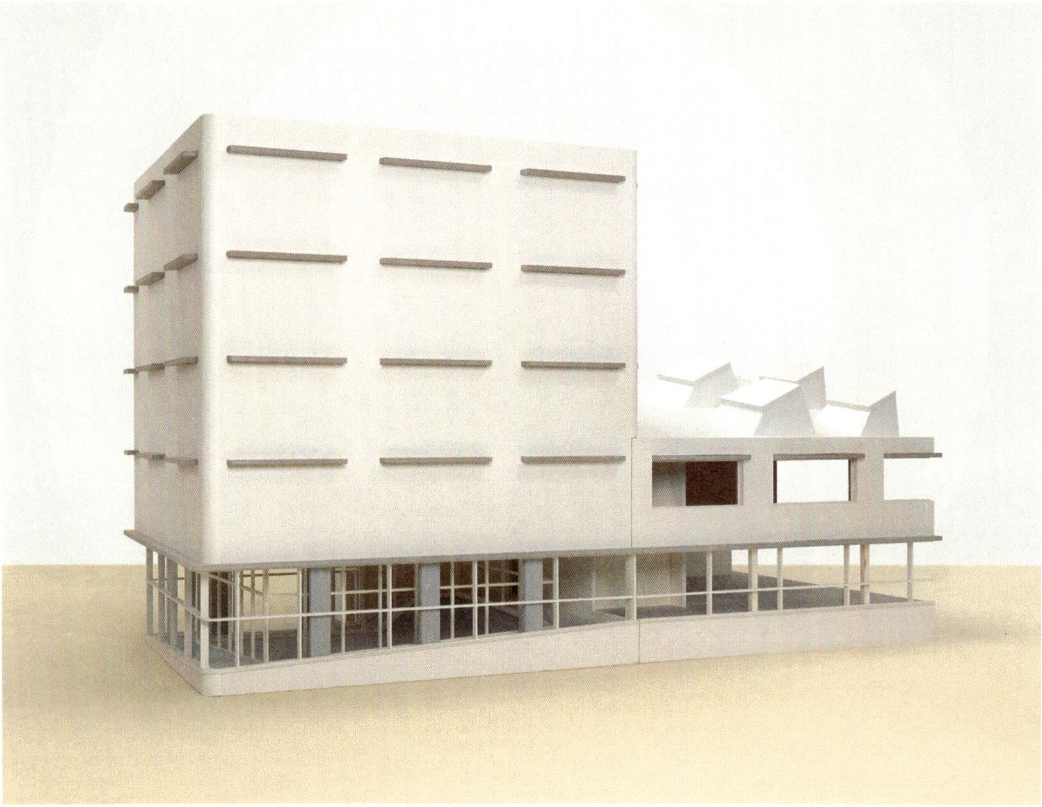

Robbrecht en Daem architecten in collaboration with Arch & Teco
State Archives Ghent

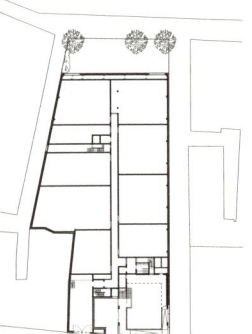

This weighty and largely blind building figure was designed by Robbrecht en Daem architecten in collaboration with Arch & Teco to house the archives in the city of Ghent. The building carefully seeks a balance between blending into the historical fabric and not shying away from standing out. The shimmering white façades and rounded corners differentiate the architecture from the neighbouring buildings. A grid of windowless windowsills gives an articulation to the blind walls, inherent to the archive programme, and makes the building enter into a dialogue with the surrounding town houses. The ground floor functions as a more public glass plinth to the blind volume on top of it. The glazed brick façades sparkle proudly in the sunlight by day, and the grid of concrete windowsills lights up subtly at night.

**STUDIOLO architectuur
in collaboration with Koen Matthys**
Walled house with winter garden

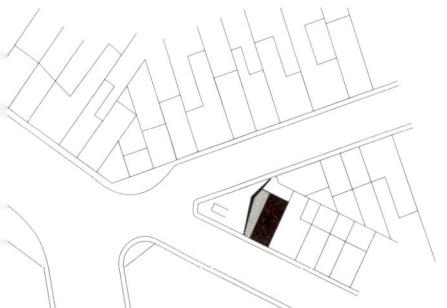

On a very steep corner in a historical working-class neighbourhood of Ghent, STUDIOLO architectuur in collaboration with Koen Matthys proposed to cut off the angle of the plot and to make a rather solid yet permeable building that is visually capable of functioning as the 'head' of the block. The brick skin does not entirely align with the insulated volume of the house, resulting in an interior volume retracted from a large part of the façade. This creates a three-storey winter garden with a mezzanine hanging in it, 'lined' in bricks. The gesture allows for very large windows in the outer skin, while maintaining a degree of privacy thanks to the buffer zone. The ambiguity of a lived interstitial space between private and public is strengthened by the encrusting of public niches and bird alcoves in the walled house's skin.

FELT architecture & design
Olijftakstraat

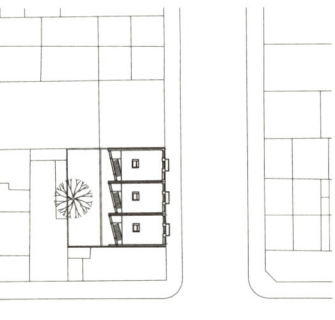

The as yet unrealized design for three similar town houses will be entirely rebuilt by FELT as three contemporary homes behind the renovated façades. The living quarters will be positioned on the upper floors so as to increase privacy, offer views over the city, and connect with the existing balconies of the façade. The architects will insert a vertical volume in the interiors. It will house all the technical facilities such as bathrooms and washing spaces, and will become a chimney-like element on the higher levels. This vertical figure was conceived as a sculpture in yellow brick that connects the stacked interior spaces and creates a coherent but varied collection of rooms.

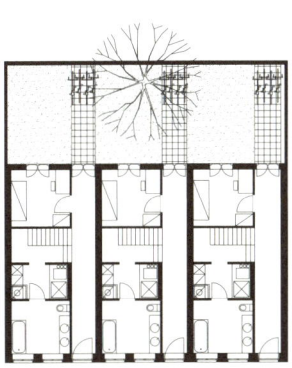
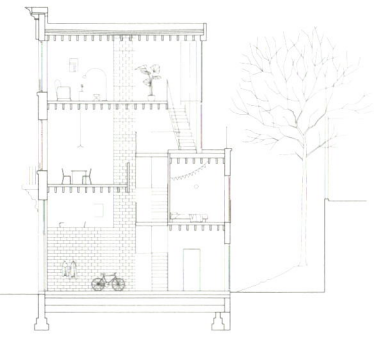

Dierendonckblancke architecten
Dambruggestraat

Dierendonckblancke architecten designed this bright apartment building on a very acute and deep plot in Antwerp. The building was conceived as a stacking of four apartments connected by an outdoor staircase. While the building marks the corner of the street with a sturdy volume, the staircase remains open, allowing for lively interaction between residents and the public sphere. By means of a split-level configuration in which the living quarters are distinguished from the night quarters, a covered outdoor bike parking was created on the ground floor. The staircase and kitchen windows give out onto a small courtyard, letting daylight into every corner of the interior.

Dierendonckblancke architecten
Twaalfkameren

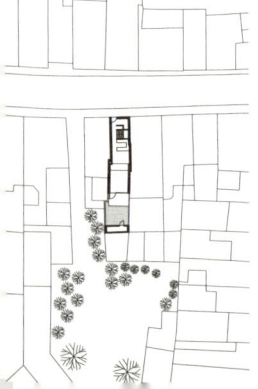

This low-budget house in the centre of Ghent was designed by Dierendonckblancke architecten in a palette of humble materials. Façades and interior spaces are largely dominated by basic concrete blocks. The simple but expressive walls were left bare or painted white, and completed with wooden ceilings, wooden stairs, nets for safety railings and ample light that enters through roof windows. The façade figures a single large window and front door, letting the concrete bricks take centre stage. The oblique roof edge finishes the composition with an equally simple but unconventional gesture.

Architecten Broekx-Schiepers
Double house Kattenberg

This double house designed by Architecten Broekx-Schiepers interweaves the two residences intimately. They meander around a circulation core that offers each of them south-facing windows and terraces. The front façade was constructed in white glazed bricks, adorned only with elaborate brick patterns at the windows and one red balcony. The side façade in turn was conceived in an industrial red brick, with a clear reference to the common blind party wall. Two sizes of bricks were used to emphasize the structure of the house and divide the façade into rectangular 'rooms' that anchor a few windows and one of the entrance doors. Without engaging in any theatricality, the building offers a restrained ending to the terraced houses, yet features some nice allusions to its context.

115

tim peeters architecten
Wolters House

The renovation of this terraced house at the edge of the city centre resulted in an inverted living situation that is embodied in the façade design. The living quarters fill the upper floors, while the night functions occupy the ground floor. This design decision is displayed in the street by a two-storey window dominating the greater part of the façade. The window and the façade composition carefully take up aspects of the original art deco-style elements on the street level. Moreover, the large window has been subdivided to meet the grain of the surrounding façades and to bridge the difference between the existing elements and the more abstract new figure of the upper balcony.

117

ono Architectuur
Prins Leopold

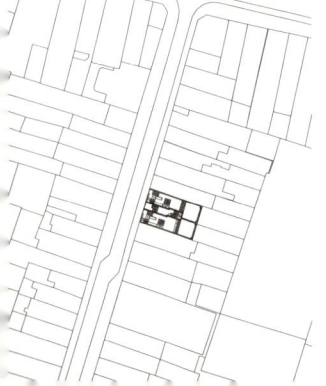

While the composition of the street façade of this passive housing project in Borgerhout suggests one smaller and one bigger residence, the street plinth presents three front doors. The plinth presents a slight tonal difference compared with the main part of the façade and is topped off with its own cornice. The cornice establishes a connection to the slightly different neighbouring terraced houses with their *piano nobile* storeys. A complex plan and section configuration entangle the three residences to create optimal living conditions on a plot theoretically too small for three terraced houses, while still offering three individual street addresses. Delicately designed mundane figures such as ventilation, drainpipes and letter boxes add depth to the monochrome façade.

DMT architecten
Meir corner building

On a corner plot of Antwerp's busiest shopping street, DMT architecten realized this residential building with a commercial plinth. The façade speaks a contemporary classic language and is rather discreet in its surroundings. Its volume, on the other hand, is more expressive. The lower floors are high, and are articulated with two-storey window bays that bring to mind a multi-legged table. The stacked apartments above form a modest corner tower that can communicate with a landmark tower nearby. This volume pulls back a little from one of the neighbouring houses, one of the last remaining sixteenth-century houses on this street. Its cornice appears appropriate on the different sides of the corner. The building tries to nuance the morphology of the city, reaching out to the different layers of time surrounding it.

Tom Thys architecten
Town hall extension, Langemark-Poelkapelle

Next to the town hall of this rural municipality, Tom Thys architecten positioned its extension almost against the existing volume, connecting them only with a hallway. The narrow space between them provides the new wing with an autonomy that is echoed in a sober but distinct architectural idiom. The sand-coloured brick feels modest next to the expressive yellow façade of the existing town hall, and the plinth height has been adopted in the new wing. A heavy white cornice adorns the building, exaggerating the existing one. The main square on the front side has been 'embraced' by rotating the façade with regard to the old town hall and by extending the cornice into a friendly welcoming canopy.

FVWW architecten
in collaboration with Dennis Tyfus
De Nor

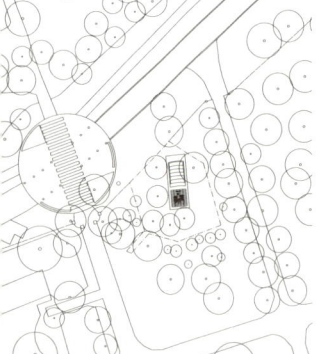

Located near the entrance of the Middelheim Museum, an open-air sculpture park in Antwerp, Frederic Vandoninck Wouter Willems architecten in collaboration with artist Dennis Tyfus realized a peculiar project that holds the middle between micro-building and scenographic device or even sculpture. The project was commissioned by the Middelheim Museum in the framework of the group show *Experience Traps*. The concrete architectural object is surrounded by a thousand-stake fence and two gates. The object itself houses a tiny bar, and appears to be a tribune from the other side. Its shape is reminiscent of an old-fashioned lock-up as much as of Aldo Rossi's Pertini monument. In all its simplicity, the peculiar construction plays out its ambiguity to the fullest.

Robbrecht en Daem architecten & Dierendonckblancke architecten in collaboration with VK Engineering & Arup
Media Building

For the design of this Media Building, the programme was roughly divided in two connected volumes: a tower volume and a slab of equal height, each on one side of an outdoor events square. Two floors of the building connect the tower with the slab and cover the square. Each façade responds to one of the facets of the park area. The long slab faces a memorial park with winter garden terraces and emphasizes the long public park running along the building. The other façades are characterized by an idiosyncratic pattern of lens-shaped windows that respond to the different park areas and views of the city. The building obtains a strong sense of autonomy, while seeming very embedded in the direct topography and context.

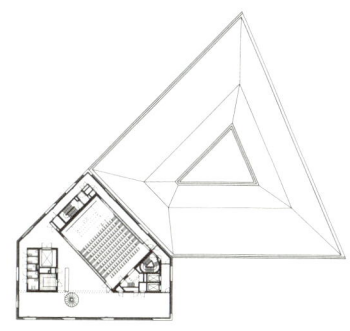

FELT architecture & design
Elementary School Zarren

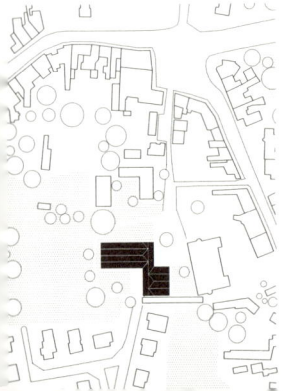

Following an Open Call procedure, FELT was selected to design a new school building in Zarren. The building comprises two wings connected by a central circulation hall and the refectory. One contains the sports hall, the other a series of classrooms. The volumes mimic the adjoining nursery with its gabled roofs. The short sides of the volumes hint at the materiality of Flemish party walls, while the long sides are rhythmic compositions in brick and concrete, topped off with red roof tiles. The windows appear to be held in place by a concrete plinth on the bottom and a greyish roof edge on top. The plinth was constructed in polished pink concrete, like the majestic staircase inside. The pink concrete returns in the playgrounds, taking the form of curved benches that pick up the playful character of the interior spaces.

Architectenbureau Bart Dehaene in collaboration with artist Dirk Zoete
Schaerdeke social housing

Architectenbureau Bart Dehaene designed this social-housing complex of 16 units around a semi-private green area. The units are paired under 'mansard roofs', a common figure in the area, reminiscent of the reconstruction architecture after the First World War. The volumes are connected by one-storey annexes and garden walls, and the corners are articulated by more compact and bent variants of the typology. Each of the corner houses has a portico that shelters the entrance of both houses, and each is adorned with a column by artist Dirk Zoete. The columns mark the end of the sightlines in the streets and are a unique sculpture for each corner. These architectural figures turn the experience of these low-cost houses into special moments.

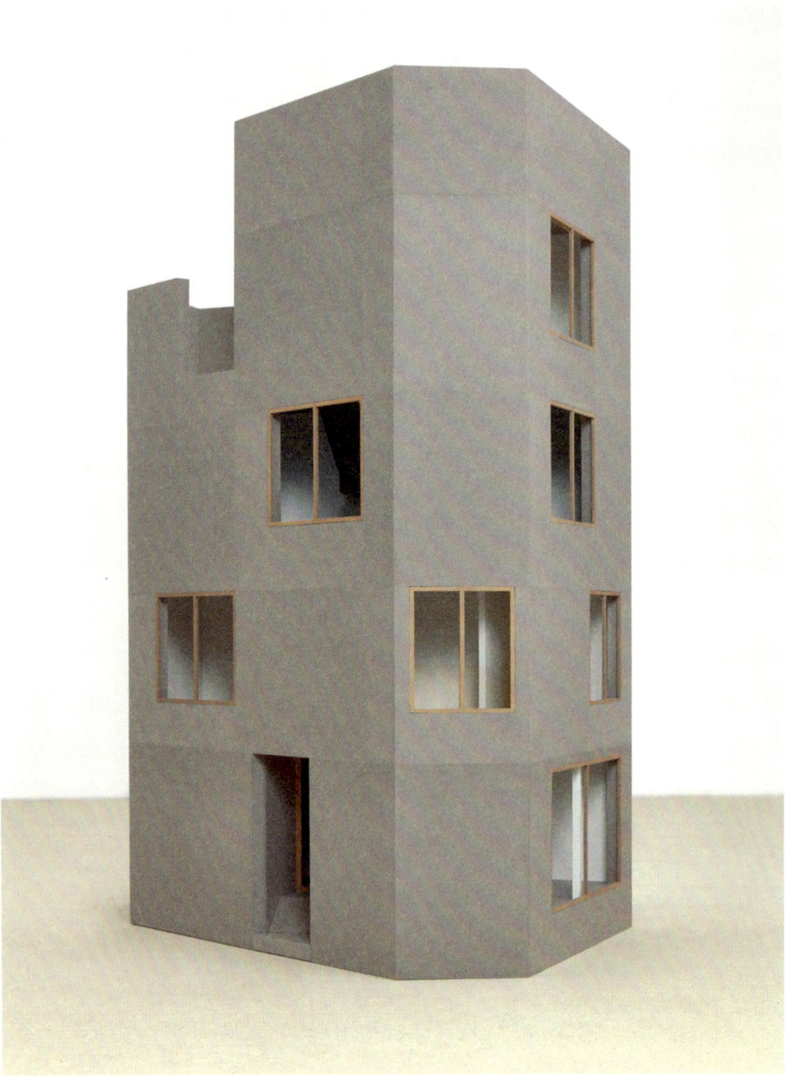

Vermeiren—De Coster Architecten
DC-V house and office

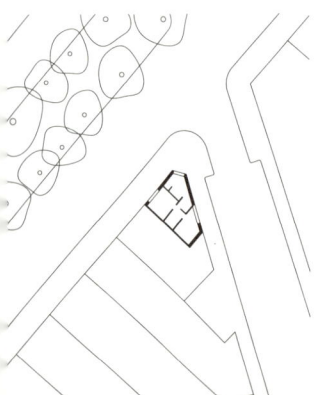

On this shallow plot on an acute corner in Antwerp, Vermeiren—De Coster Architecten refurbished this residential 'donjon' with office spaces on the ground floor. The building was divided into a sequence of rooms parallel to the large party wall so that all rooms take advantage of the street façades. The existing façades were plastered with a brush finish in two different directions, creating a chequered pattern of large rectangular surfaces that align with the edges of the windows. The raised roof edges of the living quarters on the third floor give them the appearance of an extra tower volume on the corner, next to an enclosed roof terrace. A glass pane completes the façade composition, lending the terrace a view onto the street while shielding it from the wind. These elements soften the character of this residential bunker into a friendly giant on the corner.

133

Poot Architectuur
Verzoeningstraat

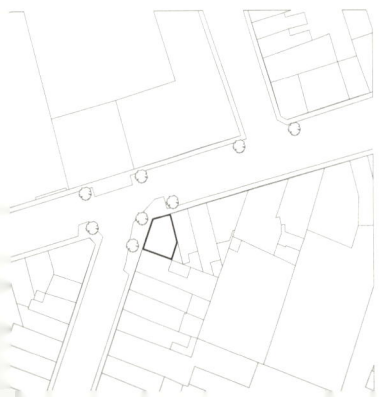

For this architect's house on a vacant corner plot, Poot Architectuur designed a straightforward brick volume that rises slightly above the neighbouring houses. With its sizeable dimensions, the house functions as a beacon on the street corner. Its materiality references the area's industrial architecture. The lack of a garden resulted in an inversion of the typology of a house. The night quarters are positioned on the lower floors, while the living area is positioned on the upper floors, closer to the roof terraces. The floors are stepped around the staircase, leading up to the equally stepped roof terrace. The clever plan and height difference between the storeys results in an interior that unfolds steadily behind the tougher and more rigid façades.

Tim Rogge Architectuur Studio
Broek

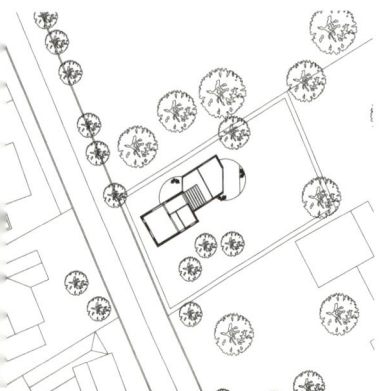

For the renovation of this house in Deurle, Tim Rogge copied the existing volume and pasted it as an extension behind it. The extension is misaligned with the existing house, emphasizing the bifold volume. It is chamfered by two large windows that open onto two circular terraces. The existing volume and the extension were unified with a new coat of bricks on which a composition was created with open and more flush joints. Inside, the space is determined by a green metal staircase and split-level floors, giving the new volume a very open and light atmosphere.

Coussée & Goris architecten
Soubry

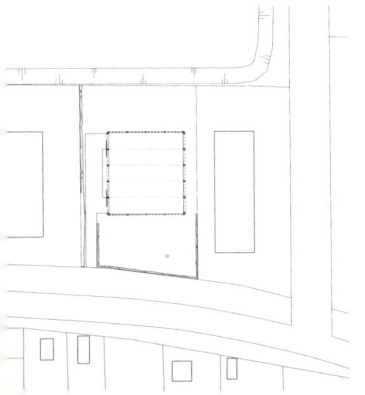

Set in an industrial area of a rural town, this carpenter's atelier with a small office space was realized by Coussée & Goris architecten. A simple flat composition, the volume was constructed following an industrial logic, with a small wooden box inside it that houses the office space. This was given a large but low window, offering views of the outside landscape and connecting with the road in front. The wooden structure of the hall defines both the interior and the façades, resulting in a rhythm of wooden pilasters that feels almost classical. Among its more recent neighbouring buildings, the hall appears highly refined yet almost invisible.

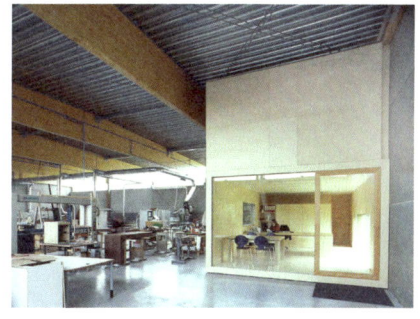

ectv architecten Els Claessens en Tania Vandenbussche
Service building container park

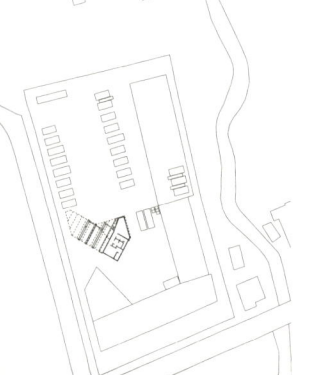

With this monochrome entrance building, ectv architecten Els Claessens en Tania Vandenbussche used a crisp gesture to structure the Jabbeke recycling centre. The construction is composed as a canopy that shelters the regulated car entrance, and a maintenance building for the centre's staff. The difference in height between the roof structure and the service building brings in extra daylight under the canopy and grants it a certain airiness. Taking its cue from the appearance of containers, the construction is clad in corrugated metal panels in a matt green hue. The sharp detailing, on the other hand, makes the building stand out from its surroundings. This interplay of referencing the mundane context while offering an autonomous architectural object that stands out renders this everyday service building unpretentiously special.

Trans architectuur stedenbouw
Ryhove Urban Factory

While located in a residential area, the factory terrain and office building that Trans architectuur stedenbouw designed for Ryhove nestles effortlessly in the grain of the surrounding fabric. The office volume was conceived in three bays perpendicular to the street, taking up a threefold gable roof that matches the scale of the terraced housing around the factory. The street façade along the first bay is robust and composed of eight equal sections, separated by slender concrete columns all the way up to the roof. These sections give the long façade a vertical character, with proportions that connect to the neighbouring terraced housing. The rigid bay rhythm was enforced by very sharp detailing that takes up a more industrial idiom. An intricate truss system adds an ornamental detail to the short end of the building.

Capricci

Dirk Somers   In addition to the *Composite Presence* scenography we invited 45 architects from around the world to make a small contribution on the matter of architectural coexistence in the contemporary city. One aisle of the Belgian pavilion displays this collection of 45 postcards, each depicting a contemporary take on the capriccio. Essentially a fictional or conceptualized cityscape, the format provides insight into what today's designers see as the city that lies ahead of us.

**Anupama
Kundoo**

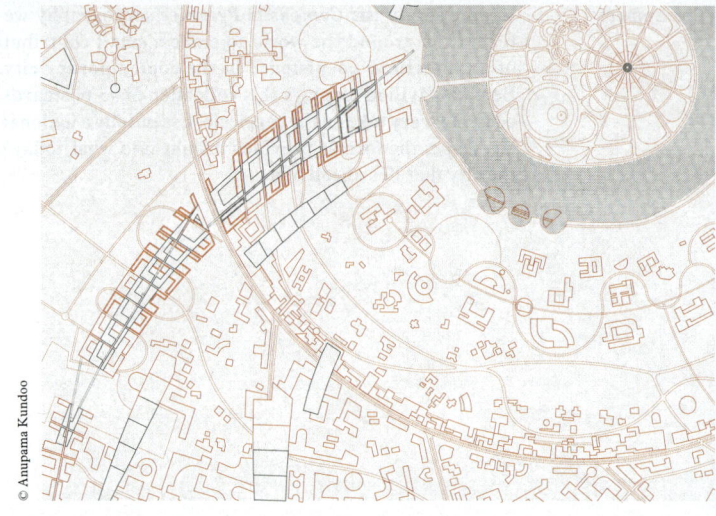

© Anupama Kundoo

**Atelier
Adam
Nathaniel
Furman**

© Adam Nathaniel Furman

**Atelier
Branco**

© Atelier Branco

Line of
Goodwill

In 1965 Mirra Alfassa, also known as The Mother, one of the leading freedom fighters in India, envisaged a new city—Auroville—dedicated to achieving human unity and international understanding, based on a vision that 'somewhere on Earth there should be a place which no nation can claim as its own, where all human beings of goodwill who have sincere aspirations can live freely as citizens of the world...' In 1965 The Mother invited French architect Roger Anger (1923–2008) to design the city. On 28 February 1968 the foundation of this city was laid, 10 km north of Pondicherry in a barren 'wasteland' with the participation of 5,000 people from 125 countries and all the Indian states, bringing a handful of earth from their homelands to a marble-clad urn in the shape of a lotus bud that still stands at the centre of this planned city.

Pride

You're trapped in their world
DOGMA & policed conformity
Mascara, smeared lipstick & semen
Involuntary Rem Koolhaas prisoners
Copious perfume, body hair and sweat
Urine stains in a John Pawson toilet
You're not allowed, they say
Bjarke Ingels alphamales
Erase yourself, is their message
A tomb of Zumthor's own making
Chiffon, tassels, face paint & tattoos
An endless Tadao Ando labyrinth
Erect nipples through printed fabrics
Trying to have fun in a Caruso St John
A handful of wet love handles
Stretchmarks, scars and Venetian fabrics
Kenneth Frampton weeps silently
While you gently whisper
David Chipperfield always looks so terribly sad

Urban
Silence

Believing in what we experienced in the cities over the last decades, and considering the lack of common sense in the practice of architecture (whether small or large scale), we are facing a disastrous form of dispersion in the denser cities. The city started to fail from its foundations and silence replaced the noise of the old urban rhythm. We believe in this very challenging process to research silence and slow the flow. Here in Brazil, nature varnishes our mistakes in cities, in Italy it is in small medieval villages. We call it 'borgo'. We feel the beauty of this change as his first with silence. What do we see in the long term? Will the wilderness allow our new cities?

bplus.xyz

© Schnepp Renou

Barozzi Veiga

© Collage by Barozzi Veiga (background photo by Axel Hütte)

baukuh

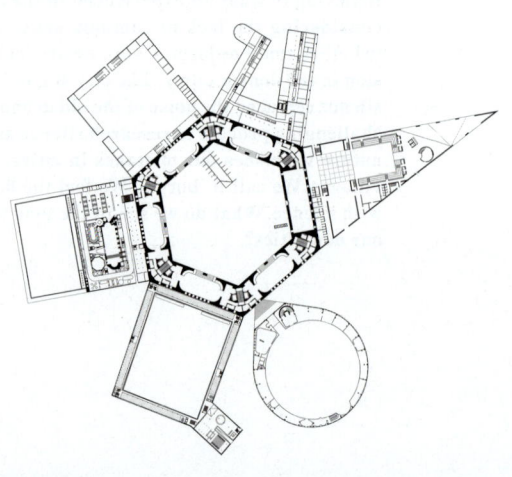

© baukuh

San Gimignano Lichtenberg: The story told today forms a future reality

In the early 2010s, Berlin Lichtenberg was still a long way off, at least in the minds of the real-estate industry ... No one could imagine an alternative use for an abandoned GDR production site on the outskirts of Berlin, let alone an investment in a 'ruin project'. Only the narrative reinterpretation gave the production site a new imaginative orientation: San Gimignano Lichtenberg. With the image of the small Tuscan town, a space of imagination opened up and hinted at the idea of a new possible future: more towers were to be built, the scenery was to be expanded ... The outcome is still uncertain, but (the future is) promising.

Venetian Capriccio at Punta della Dogana

Architecture navigates between two different realities: an ideal one, where forms and principles are pure and autonomous, and a real one, specific and contextual, hybrid and impure. Ideas move between both conditions, each feeding the other. 'A sentimental monumentality', born in the Corderie at the 2016 Biennale, now dialogues with the Renaissance columns of Punta della Dogana and with the ephemeral architecture anchored there years ago.

Asclepeion

We are broken. We need Asclepius to visit us in our dreams in the middle of the night. We need to be confined inside the temenos of an Asclepeion until we regain physical and mental health. This capriccio is a tribute to the Asclepeion as a wild accumulation of individual forms, creating a complete and separate universe. Their original meanings, their functions are transcended by the new overall composition, intended as a difficult whole. To imagine how it might look like is left to the viewer.

Bernd Schmutz Architekten

© Bernd Schmutz Architekten

Besler & Sons

© Erin Besler and Ian Besler

Brandão Costa Arquitectos

© Nuno Brandão Costa

Accumulations   A landscape of real and imagined relations, defined and loose constellations, our city mediates between scales, found situations and memories, allowing speculation, embracing past and present, stimulating experience and transformation. It is a responsive collection of differences, continuity, juxtapositions, novelty, conventions, ordinariness, surprise, greenery, contradiction, appropriation, variety, pop, refinement, imperfection, tolerance, the picturesque, chance, grandeur, lightness, gravity, reservation, animation, artefacts.

Likeable Cities   These images of charming, compelling and otherwise idiosyncratic interventions and manifestations of the messy, curious and quirky relationships between people, buildings and cities are presented here as probes, projected outward to measure the extent of inclusion in architectural and design discourse. Each entry calls out to validate and acknowledge a broader engagement with forms of knowledge that haven't been given meaningful attention or are only just emerging. As digital culture and social media allow these material and formal practices to proliferate well beyond any specific site or city, the digital mediation current with day-to-day experience is increasingly reorganizing our shared perceptions and associations, particularly between architecture and place.

East Oporto   The East Oporto capriccio is like capriccio paintings used to be. A fantasy about architecture and nature. A 480-metre-long concrete portico gallery, under construction, melts with nature, creating a textured perspective space, feeling abstract and organic. It is a drawing of hope, and when it is finished and in use, I hope it will feel somehow like this.

Buol & Zünd

Carla Juaçaba Studio

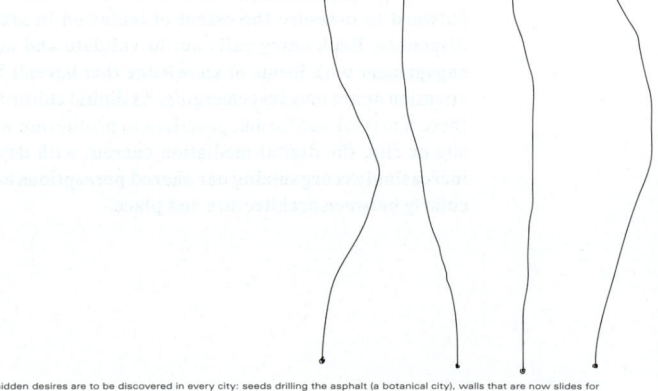

hidden desires are to be discovered in every city: seeds drilling the asphalt (a botanical city), walls that are now slides for the children (boundaries of joy), missed ágoras (free politics without media), floating libraries ('teatros del mondo'), etc.

... to be continued; to be redesigned

Charles Holland Architects

*The
Staircase*

A curious, searching observation of the artefacts that shape our everyday lives: the waiting –for an event, an appearance, a phenomenon, something that could perhaps come about spontaneously, a lighting mood, the smell of the room – is a decisive one, a design attitude towards architecture as everyday life.

Latent City

hidden desires are to be discovered in every city:
seeds drilling the asphalt
walls that are now slides for the children
missed agoras
floating libraries

a botanical city
boundaries of joy
free politics without media
'teatros del mondo'
to be continued
to be redesigned

*Looking for
a Way Out*

'The trouble began in Venice, with the back alleys.'

Antal Szerb's 1937 novel *Journey by Moonlight* describes the unravelling of a relationship during a disastrous honeymoon in Venice. But it could describe the Biennale itself and its labyrinthine detours, its loops and lay-bys and endless returns. It is perhaps impossible to imagine the new city when we are still so hopelessly lost in the old one.

Christ & Gantenbein

Cino Zucchi

Conen Sigl Architekten

We are convinced that a project never starts from scratch. On the contrary, creativity is always related to that which exists and it gains nourishment and inspiration from it.

Blossfeldt's Invaders or Ťhę Ř̄ætûrŋ ọf̧ ťḩę̧ Ģi̧ǫ̇ṅt Hōġṳɔę̣̇d̄

Trying to evoke Mother Nature's (supposed) harmonic growth, countless organic metaphors pervade last century's planning and design lexicon: under its quasi-Orwellian Newspeak, houses become 'cells', highways become 'arteries', parks become 'lungs' and the whole metropolis a 'living organism'. But rather than a single token of the animal or vegetal kingdom, the present territory resembles a complex ecosystem where individual elements replicate their own 'selfish genes' through the genetic variation of the patterns which altogether form our 'material culture'. If contemporary skyscrapers crave to become plants, Karl Blossfeldt's iconic stems aspire to become architecture, penetrating our ever-changing 'concrete jungle' like a Giant Hogweed.

Teatrino

The city as a stage. The architectonic elements, together with all kinds of inhabitants and species, are the protagonists of an ever-evolving play. Protagonists get off the scene, some things are rearranged and modified. There are niches and places to stay, dwell, nest and watch the play. But there are also places that are an invitation to gather, act and become an active part in the microcosm of the city. Plays are rewritten and reinterpreted.

**David Kohn
Architects**

© David Kohn Architects

DRDH

© DRDH

**False
Mirror
Office**

© False Mirror Office

London 2121   After 'The discovery of the temple of Isis at Pompeii, buried under pumice and other volcanic matter'. Coloured etching by Pietro Fabris, 1776, in *Campi Phlegraei* by Sir William Hamilton (1730–1803), a copy of which is in Sir John Soane's collection. Soane had personally scaled Mount Vesuvius in January 1779.

A Tragicomic City, after Serlio   In 1545 Serlio first proposed the city as a scenography in which life could play out as theatre: the comic city of everyday buildings alongside the tragic city of noble edifices, and finally the satiric, enshrouded by forest. He commended his readers to elaborate upon those sketches and we have taken the cue. Our contemporary scene draws together comedy, tragedy and satire. Here good, ordinary buildings rub shoulders with the civic, the civil and the collective. This borrowed architecture, made by women and men, by friends, is part of an ecology. Leaving space for diverse nature, it is a city that has learned from the recent past, where statues remain toppled and animals range freely. It is somewhat messy and unresolved, as the ideal city should be.

The Architect's Dream   The contemporary architect no longer faces the historical city centre, which he or she is basically banned from, but the peripheral and industrial areas. The ordinary, monotonous volumes of the suburbs often host the most avant-garde and experimental activities, also banned from the inner city. Today, *The Architect's Dream* is to transform these suburban silent structures into new monuments that translate the identity of these brilliant activities into a fantastic set of signifying figures, decorative billboards, platonic-phallic forms, animalier epiphytes and colossal objets trouvés.

**Feina
Studio**

© Feina Studio

**Hans van
der Heijden
Architect**

© Hans van der Heijden Architect

**Hild und K
Architekten**

© Collage HILDUNDK

Sous les pavés, la plage

Social revolt as a model for de-urbanization. A literal interpretation gives rise to a radical potential evoking lost memories and reconnecting society with the landscape. A non-distant utopia, where selective de-urbanizaton is foreseen—a way of reclaiming lost porous natural ground while beautifully bringing social justice.

Our Love of Boring Things

Arguably, the palazzo is the most sophisticated housing type—in any case it is the most overlooked one. Because it could not be otherwise, Naples grew in the eighteenth century predominantly through speculatively built palazzi. The architectural variation which is celebrated within that type contributes to the intriguing vitality of Naples. The city is an object lesson for those who esteem the classification of Boring Things.

Anchored

The architecture relates to its context. It references history but progresses by creatively reinterpreting technical methods, treatments or changes of materials. The combination of modern technical possibilities and traditional craftsmanship leads to a location-dependent architecture. This architecture is rooted in our time and refers to the existing vernacular. The collage raises the question: 'To what extent do the buildings still relate to their original context when placed in new surroundings?'

Junya Ishigami + Associates

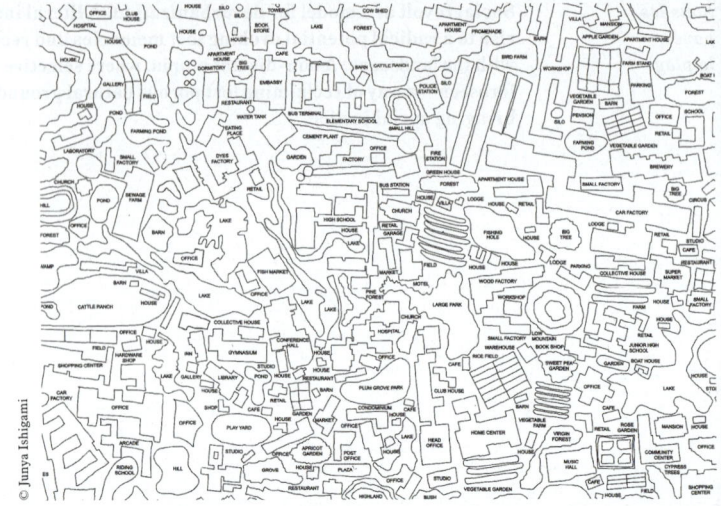

Johansen kovsted Arkitekter

Jean-Benoît Vétillard

Blending Environment

The city has neither centre nor periphery, neither beginning nor end; there is no distinction between what is infrastructure and what is not, nor any boundary between artificial and natural. It is an environment with a variety of forms and relationships that far exceeds the scale of existing cities, accepts all things, allows all things to flow, and freely blends together. No longer able to call this a 'city' (a place that is solely planned for people to live in), we can only refer to it as an 'environment' (an expansion that is both for and not for people).

The Construction Site is Like a City

The construction site is like a city. In a perpetual state of change. A system of components (people) in a latent condition. Assemblage or conflict? A coexistence between the landscape and (ruinous) layers of settlement. Full of life or left for a moment.

Trapissier Vénitien

In Osteria della Rivetta I met a Venetian upholsterer who used to photograph his creations—beds, sofas, armchairs, etc.—in the street near his workshop before delivering them to their owners. This is where he found the perfect and necessary light for the archiving of his work.

Linghao Architects

© Fabian Ong

A Sunday morning. The three children crouch over the entrance garden of gravel stones, bananas, gingers, pandans, marigolds … Dexterously, they extricate caterpillars and throw them into pails of water. Will it work? The previous weekend, the family devised a folding blind system out of straw mats, hanging them over the outdoor sink. Settling into the house is like slowly fleshing out how and what and where they should be in relation to this and that. Four weeks after moving in, the gourds are fruiting and the spinach leaves are being obliterated by a sea of caterpillars. Will they become a sky of butterflies? Doing the laundry at the innermost corner of the interior, a gentle breeze is suddenly felt. The ever-renewing freshness is the perpetual reinvention of the monsoon or local winds. Even at this remote corner, the air flows. Left to accumulate, the house will be quickly filled with 10 bamboo poles of laundry hung out to dry. No wonder the popularity of the dry-fit T-shirt with the family and almost everybody, breathable and designed to naturally dry. After starting the family and living here for the previous 8 years, this remaking of this house was also a finding out of what could be a comfortable house, in what could be a natural way to go about everyday. Rainwater coming in and leaving puddles that would dry up would be in this vein. These openings also bring in the sunlight, the night streetlights, the freely flowing wind from a different direction and intensity at each time, the chatter of the passers-by, to be part of the house world. So far, this means walking carefully when the floor is wet, living with the caterpillars and aphids, treasuring the sounds of the hanging pots and pans clanging against each other in the quiet and windy night, playing on the smartphone while doing the homework on the timber corridor in the shade of the house while feeling the wind.

Madeleine Kessler and Manijeh Verghese, Unscene Architecture

© Madeleine Kessler and Manijeh Verghese, Unscene Architecture

MAIO

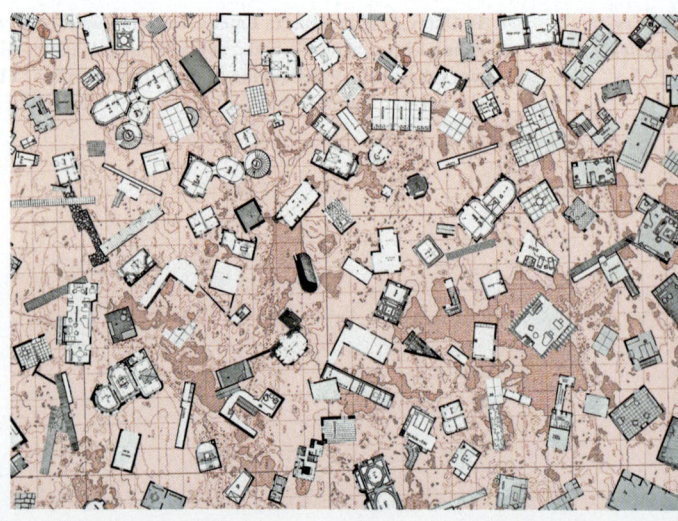

© MAIO

Compound A Sunday morning. The three children crouch over the entrance garden of
House   gravel stones, bananas, gingers, pandans, marigolds ... Dexterously, they
           extricate caterpillars and throw them into pails of water. Will it work?
           The previous weekend, the family devised a folding blind system out of
           straw mats, hanging them over the outdoor sink. Settling into the house is
           like slowly fleshing out how and what and where they should be in relation
           to this and that. Four weeks after moving in, the gourds are fruiting and
           the spinach leaves are being obliterated by a sea of caterpillars. Will they
           become a sky of butterflies?

The Middle *The Middle Ground* explores the relationship between private and public
Ground   spaces in the city, looking at how we can better open up spaces for the
              public and give communities greater agency and ownership over their
              public spaces. The collage is part of a triptych looking at how architects,
              developers, politicians, citizens and legislators are constantly navigating
              between the utopia of the commons and the dystopia of total privatization.

The Diffuse The diffuse house is ubiquitous. The diffuse house operates 24/7. The diffuse
House   house is networked. The diffuse house does not necessarily manifest itself
               under a new form or typology, although it does not exclude it. The diffuse
               house is the new archetypal form of domestic space. The diffuse house is
               a factory. The diffuse house is an office, a workstation, a workshop and
               a home. The diffuse house relies on immaterial economies. The diffuse
               house is post-Fordist. The diffuse house constitutes the germ of the 'Grand
               Interior', the continuous spatial core of late capitalism.

Mark Pimlott

Mary Duggan

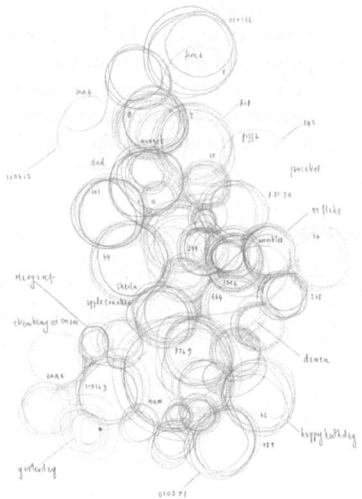

Matteo Ghidoni— Salottobuono

Piazza Delle Distanze   The Piazza del Duomo in Orvieto—which sets the city's most significant space in sight of its landscape and offers tenderness in all its aspects, from sacred to profane, and accommodates the contributions of its citizens across ages—provides the framework for other protagonists in this 'capriccio'. Some have been called from other cities, their scales changed in order to fit the clothes of the piazza's true inhabitants; others are inventions that have never been realized; others still are foreign bodies, likely to leave or be welcomed, depending on their own humility.

Memory Map   I travel through my mind in search of my deepest, most significant and important memories…. The pencil line recalls and searches back and forth at my pace in my headspace. The numbers and words extract the pertinent mark within easy reach—a collage of landline numbers, mobile phones, door numbers, marathon distances, births and deaths, brothers, sisters, boyfriends, people and tastes. The space they create is of course imaginary, but from it I extract a city within my proximity as a reflection. It is close to me. It is my scope. I imagine our future city from such a position—close, accessible—a city that can host life and livelihood through large and small gestures, both fast and slow.

Belonging to the Mediterranean Coast   Proposal: mixed-use building.
Programme: hotel, offices, apartments, retail, leisure, parking.
Gross floor area: 160,000 m^2.

Monadnock

© Monadnock + Garance Weber

Muoto

© Muoto

NOMOS

© NOMOS

A View From We often wonder which model of Serlio offers the more appealing setting for our architecture. For this occasion we chose the comic setting in which variety, duality and accidentism allow us to celebrate the individuality and simultaneity of objects forming an urban scenery. As learned from *Collage City*, a city of fragments challenges our conventions by offering spontaneous relations and configurations caused by strong characters positioned close to each other, explorations which urge us yet again to strive for articulated and pronounced architecture, offering various readings and layers of interpretation.

Stockton Dear all, we've just arrived. The city looks like a mixture of other cities. Rotterdam, Athens, Montreal and Tokyo seem to have melted together. Northern winds, quiet people, red and blue faces. Gentle chaos and a sweet smell of pollution. The sky is always white. Water tanks on the roofs. Cars on every floor. Modern buildings next to medieval streets too tight for the limousine. Cheers

Duet Acting Distances dwindle and swell between Geneva and Madrid: we like to think that swings, oscillations and jumps are part of our work tools as architects. Over the years, we have developed space in our offices to communicate with each other—a ceiling camera linked up to a video conference allowing us to draw side by side: ideas and forms travel from one city to the other. We strongly believe in the fruitful coexistence of lively differences.

Noreile Breen

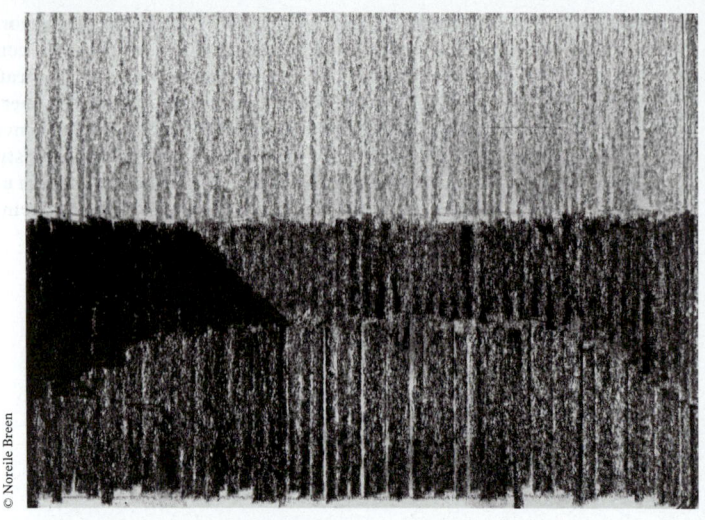

© Noreile Breen

OMMX

© OMMX

Point Supreme Architects

© Point Supreme Architects

What is the spatial possibility of the city?

My capriccio is a perspective drawing of a space in which we stand. There is a floor, three walls and, with the presence of a sharp shadow of the sun, the sky. Nothing exists {?} beyond the walls. There is no ground, no horizon, no landscape, no trees, no buildings.

A Second Shot

A Second Shot takes aim at architecture's inertia in responding to human needs. It depicts the domestic spaces and objects we have come to rely on during the pandemic. At its epicentre is a tabletop: a window on the world outside where our chaotic lives now unfold. A crumbling totem, formed from the spaces that have kept us connected, signals yet another opportunity to change course and avert disaster. The city beyond is rendered as both a flattened memory and canvas, as we all prepare to emerge, having received our second shot of coronavirus vaccine. *A Second Shot* was produced in homage to Aldo Rossi's *L'Architettura Assassinata*.

How will we live together, Athens
(Tribute to Spyros Vassiliou)

Athens is a city made of people, with small buildings, small houses, without big parks or grand streets. It is very dense and domestic, like a large village. Doors frequently open, life flows outside, chairs are placed on the pavement, marble doorsteps become wide seating areas. Families, generations, neighbourhoods, together—watching, playing, cooking, sharing. There's no difference between inside and outside, private and public, streets and living rooms. Living together means making the city together, forever, constructing, sharing, appropriating, enjoying. The city as your house, the house as the city, imperfect, permanently unfinished, with pride, memory, a sense of celebration, always.

With the support of the Graham Foundation for Advanced Studies in the Fine Arts

Sam Jacobs

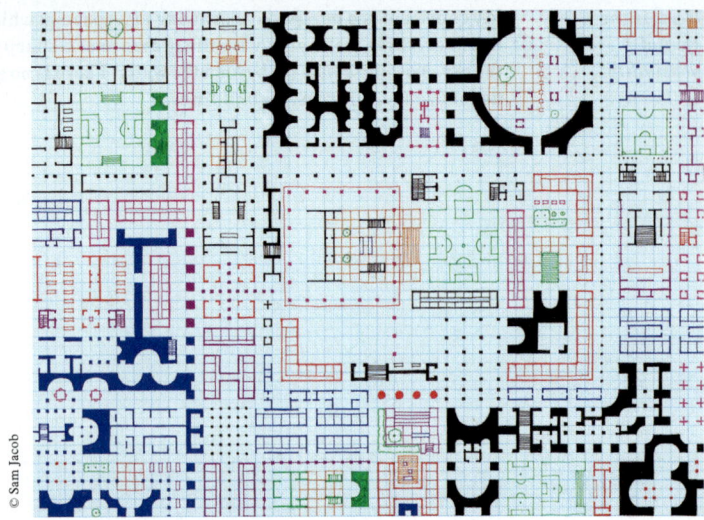
© Sam Jacob

PROLOG

© Rafał Śliwa

Klaus
Schäfer,
Hochschule
Bremen,
Institut
der Stadt-
baukunst

© Klaus Schäfer, Hans Schimansky

Empire of Ice Cream

What is the European city but an accidental capriccio? Not one produced as a singular dream of an auteur—instead, by the collective action of history. Ruins and fragments. Thwarted plans. Things that remain yet serve other ends. Not history per se, but inherited remnants. This is context, should you choose to accept it. These series of drawings are formed by remembered parts, banal contemporary elements, grand fragments, and are made as doodles across the graph paper. Edge to edge it forms an incoherent, mindless-yet-rational system (perhaps as the city itself is produced), forming a non-romantic, anti-celebratory capriccio.

A View from Outside

For quite a long time, critics have been at the centre of our gaze, thus representation and practice. The countryside was left in the periphery. The incomprehensible scale of rural areas sparked the imagination of the landscape, yet in reality made them the grey zone in relation to the cityscape. Perhaps there is a possibility to reimagine the city today by looking at it from the outside. Once we erase them from the territory, we are able to shift the gaze towards the periphery in order to see better cities again.

Archetypes of Urban Design

The Institute of Civic Arts is conceived as a forum for academic discussion on the architecture of the city. The term 'civic arts' will be clearly formulated and the scope of its application will be deliberately limited to the manifest image of the city. The general (relativist) discourse on the term 'urban' is not an issue here. The goal—the dense, mixed and compact city—is a comprehensive one. The aim is to approach the essence of the city definitively, from different perspectives, and to explore the spatial, structural, sociological and economic aspects of these observations. The city will be translated from a retrospective image into a future programme—learning from the existing substance!

Studio Bua

Studio Donna van Milligen Bielke & Ard de Vries Architecten

Studio Ossidiana

Cities and Signs 1

'You walk for days among trees and among stones. Rarely does the eye light on a thing, and then only when it has recognized that thing as the sign of another thing: a print in the sand indicates the tiger's passage; a marsh announces a vein of water; the hibiscus flower, the end of winter. All the rest is silent and interchangeable; trees and stones are only what they are.... Outside, the land stretches, empty, to the horizon; the sky opens, with speeding clouds. In the shape that chance and wind give the clouds, you are already intent on recognizing figures: a sailing ship, a hand, an elephant...'
—From *Invisible Cities* by Italo Calvino (translated from the Italian by William Weaver)

In-Between

Architecture casts the space around us. Ultimately, this is more important than what is usually the primary reason to build—to produce the required square metres for a certain functional need. A building's function is less significant than its dialogue with its immediate context. Together with other edifices, a building determines the architectural borders of the public space. This public space is comprised of streets, alleys, courts and squares, which form the interlocked public network, the urban warp and weft which give a city its structure, character and usability. In essence, our architecture is about making boundaries, by subdividing space through borders, by making the decisions between interior and exterior, private and public, open and closed. In this sense, our architecture is concentrated in the confines between distinct worlds. To a significant extent, our work is defined by a condition of the in-between, which occurs where building and city, architecture and urbanism meet.

The City of Birds

Birds populate our metaphors, inform our music and language, appear in allegories and myths from the foundation of cities to the origin of speech ... From crops to weapons, music to faith, birds are in our thoughts, in our diet, in our songs. The *City of Birds* is a collection of models, ranging from dovecotes to aviaries, bird feeders to perches, bat towers to bird cages, portraying a fictional 'city of birds' born from the devices, spaces and objects people invented to mediate the encounter between our species and another. At times tender, at times violent and simplistic, they tell the story of caloric, spiritual and cultural ties which bind us to other species.

Studio Sergison

Veldwerk Architecten

Zvi Hecker

An Image of Zurich, 2040

Between 2017 and 2020, Studio Sergison, at the Academy of Architecture in Mendrisio, invested in a study that considered what Zurich might look like in 25 years' time. While this task considered how a projected population increase of 100,000 people could be managed in urban and architectural terms, and at least 108 sites were identified in the city for a process of densification, the image of the city remains largely intact ... This image of Zurich in 2040 inserts many of the projects that the students developed over six semesters.

Wiener Festwochen

This capriccio was dreamt up by the computer. It builds upon research into incidental space conducted for the Gebäudelehre Chair at the RWTH in Aachen. The structures shown are constructed using a digital neural network that dreams up a whole new assembly of Gothic interpretations of industrial structures made in 2019 by the students. Rather than ruination by weathering, it presents a new way of constructing incidental space. Very much fitting to the idea of the capriccio as an architectural fantasy, placing together buildings, ruins and other fictional elements. The project's title, *Wiener Festwochen*, and the image description, were dreamt up by a second neural network that was fed a short narrative based on the brief.

Neuer Platz am Brandenburger Tor

On urbanism: Comparing the results of nineteenth-century expansion of all the major European cities with the spread and enlargement of those cities in the twentieth century, it is obvious that the latter work was done by architects unprepared for the task. Paris, Barcelona, Vienna, Moscow, Madrid and Berlin were enlarged in the nineteenth century by architects who possessed the required expertise, the wide technical knowledge of and inventiveness to incorporate new technologies like sewage and gas within the urban fabric, with radio, telephone, electricity and trams following close behind. Those were revolutionary changes and look how well they were incorporated. Even today, the plans of Baron Haussmann in Paris and of Ildefons Cerdà in Barcelona provide us with great examples ...

Canaletto, Capriccio View with Palladio's Design for the Rialto Bridge, 1742

Building a Middle Ground, 9 Voices

Maarten Van Den Driessche

A considerable share of the projects shown in this model landscape took shape within a specific cultural-policy context designed to give good architecture a chance. Compared to an almost non-existent architectural culture in the recent past, a genuine cultural shift was introduced in Flanders around the turn of the century. Today, it is no longer one body that determines the architectural scene. Nor is it one government architect, but several. And it is not one centralized bureaucratic organization, but a scattered group of institutions with their own mode of operation and their own local anchoring.

In this growing process of institutionalization, the Flemish Government Architect is an important, but certainly not the only link. Today, city architects are active in places such as Ghent, Brussels and Antwerp. At other administrative levels—cities and municipalities, regions and provinces, within regional and inter-municipal partnerships—building aesthetics committees, urban workshops and 'quality chambers' have been set up or revitalized. Some organizations had been in existence for a long time already and underwent a process of transformation. Others were created recently. Still others are present *in nuce*.

We can speak of a genuine proliferation of related institutions that are here somewhat broadly called 'quality chambers'. Such a chamber organizes a discussion about architectural quality at an early stage of the design process, when adjustments can easily be made. These chambers provide non-binding advice; the legislation in force comes first. The discussion is therefore not exclusively determined by legislative frameworks and legal processes. Figures with authority—with the right knowledge and expertise—mediate the conversation. Lastly, the mode of operation of the quality chambers demonstrates that the debate has to be entered into systematically, on a case by case basis.

In this story, government architects act as middlemen. 'What the Government Architect does is to facilitate the meeting. [...] The Government Architect, devoted to the public interest and at home in architecture, is ideal to open the debates. Then the dynamics of the meeting take over. The couples take shape and the middleman disappears from the stage. [...] It is the usual actors, a client and an architect, who have to get the job done.'[1] Because government architects open but do not close the debates, introduce meetings, but also disappear from the stage at the opportune time, on the one hand their merit is very tangible, but on the other hand the result cannot be attributed to them unilaterally. The search for quality cannot be reduced to a standard formula, but gains from gathering broader support and the necessary opposition.[2]

Quality chambers play an important part in the development of the architectural landscape as we know it today. They are locally embedded, but also form a finely ramified and interconnected learning network that takes on a different form according to the circumstances. Fundamental preparatory work is carried out by local administrations and city services. Research institutes and specialized design offices provide advice and carry out design research. Future clients are guided and their ambitions strengthened, but sometimes also they are slowed down or contradicted. Mediating structures and civil-society organizations participate in the discussion, but offer resistance at regular intervals. The chambers sometimes serve the general public and as such receive complaints or face urgent societal challenges; at other times they set the agenda and steer.

Under the name 'quality chamber', we have gathered people who have assumed the role of middleman in the discussion room. Thus, the voices collected here are not 'master puppeteers', but representatives of a broader culture of negotiation and discussion. The editors of this publication invited them because they each, in different capacities and within different institutional contexts, have coloured architectural policy.

---

[1] Vermeulen, P. (2011). 'Doorzichtige Dingen' in: Bouwmeesterrapport 2010–2011. Brussels: Team Vlaams Bouwmeester, p.106.

[2] In this relation, see the central part of our exhibition: Liefooghe, M., Van Den Driessche, M. et al. (2019). Open Oproep. 20 jaar Architectuur in Publieke Opdracht. Exh. cat. Brussels: Team Vlaams Bouwmeester; and the interview in: Devoldere, S. and Ngo, A.-L. (2015) 'Learning from Flanders' in: Arch+ Zeitschrift für Architektur, 220, pp. 66–70.

9 Voices

Mediating is designing

'In Flanders 2020 there is no lack of interesting architecture: relevant, remarkable, high-quality ... Congratulations to the designers. But other actors also made a crucial contribution. They can be brought together under the term "architectural mediators" or "mediators in architecture", gathered around, among others, the Flemish Government Architect. Without these "mediators", forthcoming issues of the *Flanders Architectural Review* risk having to pad out the scarce architecture with militant essays, as in the early issues. This raises certain questions. Aren't many mediators in fact co-authors of Flanders' better architecture? If we think of several project leaders from local administrations—not infrequently, women architects—we can say that this is in fact the case. Mediators' work is architectural work. Mediating is designing.

Architectural mediators operate across the entire design and construction process, in the midst of a tangle of tensions: between need and policy, research and design, client and design, design and design, design and realization, public and design... Architectural mediators focus not on compromise but on the search for coalition and convergence, on the realization of the best possible conditions, beyond current expectations. Preparatory work in relation to policy needs such mediation. But architectural mediators thrive best in the bustle of a daring project procedure in which policymakers, clients, experts of various kinds, designers and the public interact, guided by a strong design and with a view to realization. Isn't such real but daring project work the *missing link* in the Flemish Government Architect's overall mission of mediation?

There is high-quality contemporary architecture that finds aesthetic inspiration in the upgrading of the fragmented Flemish space, an after-effect of Bekaert's essay on poetry and the commonplace. There is high-quality design

André Loeckx is emeritus professor in the Department of Architecture, Urban Design and Spatial Planning at KU Leuven. He is a member of the Council of Government Architects, the board of experts that has met regularly since 2011 to support critically the objectives and actions of the Flemish Government Architect. His academic activities centre on spatial change processes, urban development and architectural theory. From 2002 to 2018 he was chairman of the Flemish Community's jury and Quality Chamber for urban renewal projects. He was one of the driving forces behind the urban policy which came into force in Flanders at the turn of the century.

research that perceives the utopian contours of a horizontal metropolis in the Flemish space as a habitat of integral sustainability and circular coexistence. Neither moves policy and public towards an effective programme that responds to social-spatial needs such as climate recovery, redistribution of wealth and democratic renewal. Architectural mediation can go a third way: not the middle course of the so-called realistic support base, but a steeper and more performative path of radical revision that starts out from the things that are there. In the first place, this requires a programmatic adjustment of architecture and building. This does not have to be wrapped up in fashionable sustainability jargon. A daring new architecture, forged in the process of mediation, is the best herald of a radical revision: presentable, tangible, responsive, liveable.'

Messy spatial planning

'When I was appointed as the fourth Flemish Government Architect in 2016, the foundations of the position were laid. There was an efficient mode of operation, firmly rooted in the administration at the Flemish level. There was a smooth-running Government Architect Team. My predecessors had developed good instruments such as the Open Call and the Pilot Projects, where clustered and urgent social assignments were addressed through design research. Meaningful steps had already been taken. In my opinion, only the relationship between architecture and spatial planning remained neglected in the story about architectural quality.

The messy spatial planning in Flanders has a huge impact on the current social system: economically, ecologically, but also socially. At the start of my tenure, together with the Government Architect Team, I consulted on feasible but more large-scale transitions with regard to the use of space, spatial densification, nature management, energy production in housebuilding, affordable housing at good locations, the backlog in terms of social housing, etc. These themes coloured our long-term programme.

In Flanders there is a strong belief in the field knowledge of local authorities. At the same time, many municipalities are small and do not always have the competences to initiate complex spatial transformation processes. That is why we also conceived the 'Government Architect Scan', which explores the strengths and weaknesses of municipalities. Together with inter-municipal organizations, we created mobile quality chambers that support small municipalities in their quality policy. In places that can be densified in terms of facilities and public transport, the importance of architectural and housing quality is increasing drastically.

Leo Van Broeck held the position of Flemish Government Architect between 2016 and 2020. He is a civil engineer and architect and a co-founder of Bogdan & Van Broeck, a Brussels-based architectural firm that focuses strongly on research and distinguishes itself through its active social commitment. He has been active as a design assistant at KU Leuven since 1995 and as a professor of architectural and urban design since 2006. In 1997 he founded the non-profit association 'Stad en Architectuur' (City and architecture). In addition, Van Broeck was chairman of the Royal Federation of Architects' Associations of Belgium (FAB) from 2013 to 2016.

Awareness-raising and good communication constitute a second link in this broader transition process. The conversation about architecture is often only conducted by the happy few, by the public attending architecture exhibitions. I found that we also needed to reach the people in the street. Local authorities can only act decisively if they have the necessary backing among their supporters. Together with film-maker Nic Balthazar, we made the educational film "Plannen voor Plaats" (Planning for place), which was widely screened. I went around the region and gave lectures in venues ranging from theatres with a seating capacity of 1600 to back rooms that could barely squeeze in 40 people. In short, I wanted to increase the government architect's reach.'

'Weiterbauen' on the diffuse city

'My Berlin background largely determined my vision of the city. The ideas developed in Berlin during the *Internationale Bauausstellung* in 1987 would form the basis for decades of the *"Kritische Rekonstruktion"* of Berlin under the leadership of the then city architect (*Senatsbaudirektor*) Hans Stimmann.

My vision of Antwerp is based on the conviction that the critical-reconstruction approach forms an excellent repertoire for the transformation of the inner city and the nineteenth-century belt. In this sense, I have translated the German *"weiterbauen"*, which was originally used as an architectural principle, into an urban planning concept. However, the challenge in Antwerp does not lie so much in the nineteenth-century belt, for which we know the ingredients and recipes. It is the morphologically much less unambiguously defined "diffuse city" of the twentieth-century belt and the ring zone for which we need to develop new ideas.

This is where the opportunities for growth and urbanistic matters lie which we will have to provide an answer for in the coming years. The city has turned its back on the "dirty" ring and we are now bearing the consequences. The complexity requires a customized approach. As city architect, I can rely on a rich range of instruments, the legacy of my predecessors. The competition procedures are fashioned and refined in such a way that quality is the decisive argument in the choice of an architect. We can speak of an "Antwerp school" of architects who fit successfully in this competition tradition. In addition, design research has gained a lot of ground in recent years.

These instruments will play an important role in today's quality control. Nevertheless, in my opinion there is need for further integration of the various disciplines. That is why we have transformed the building aesthetics committee into the comprehensive quality chamber that is about more than just the visual

Christian Rapp has been City Architect of Antwerp since 2016. He was trained as a bricklayer and studied architecture at TU Berlin and TU Delft. In 1997 he was awarded the Maaskant Prize for young architects. After various visiting lectureships, he has taught at TU Eindhoven as Professor of Rational Architecture since 2007. Together with his wife Birgit he founded Rapp+Rapp in 1999. Rapp+Rapp's work has a predilection for sound buildings, the use of traditional materials, and the making of architectural urbanism.

quality or the architecture of projects. This will be the platform where all the expertise in terms of urban planning, architecture, public space and heritage will come together to discuss the major urban issues—I am thinking of the roofing-over projects of "De Grote Verbinding" (The Big Link)—as well as the strategies for the climate-robust city.'

Quality always deserves a good conversation

'Those who know Brussels a little know that its cityscape is not a model of harmony. Brussels is not a cute city, but a very diverse city in many aspects. Brussels is administratively complex. The Brussels-Capital Region is made up of 19 municipalities with considerable administrative autonomy. Brussels is an independent region within the federal state structure, but also the capital of Belgium, of Flanders and of Europe. The Flemish and French-speaking communities have powers in the capital. On the administrative level, there are so many layers that we jokingly call it the "Brussels lasagna". Hundreds of thousands of commuters come to work in Brussels every day, without making this city their home. European expats stay in Brussels temporarily and settle there provisionally because of their work. The population is growing rapidly. Because only 1 in 3 Brussels residents have both parents of Belgian nationality, it is the most socially diverse city in Europe. The architectural diversity of the cityscape actually reflects the complexity of my city. I see Brussels as a laboratory of the future European city, because the conditions of complexity will persist in many places.

In this complexity, the position of Government Architect, which has been in existence in Brussels since 2009, is finding a position of its own. The general objective of my function is to promote spatial quality in the new urban projects and that therefore also requires the necessary decisiveness to do away with all kinds of old-school practices that have not always benefited the city's urban development in the past. Because the government architect can work independently of politics and administration, it is eminently possible to focus on transversal cooperation, which connects horizontally between different administrative silos, professional disciplines and design scales. Because the government architect belongs to no one, he can work with anyone.

Kristiaan Borret has been the Government Architect of the Brussels-Capital Region since 2015. He began a second term in 2020. He has been a guest professor at Ghent University since 2005. From 2006 to 2014 he was City Architect of Antwerp. Throughout his career he has moved between theory and practice, between public and private sector, between policy and design. He has carried out research into the contemporary transformations of the city, urbanity and public space. As a designer he has worked on various urban designs, infrastructure studies and public-space projects. In 2013 he received the Culture Prize for Architecture of the Flemish Community.

In the course of 2015, I introduced a quality chamber in Brussels to discuss architectural projects before they are submitted as building applications. After all, the earlier in the design process you can influence the design quality, the easier it is to accept and effectively improve the project. I believe it is an essential role of the government architect to ensure that a discussion about spatial quality takes place at all, and also in a decent, transparent and well-founded manner. That's what the quality chamber is for.

Since 2019, the principle of a quality chamber has been incorporated into Brussels spatial-planning legislation. While the quality chamber is now anchored in terms of the participation of all the public stakeholders concerned, I believe that the new challenge is to expand the circle of discussion. Making the city is no longer done by traditional bodies alone, but by a broad constellation of city-makers in a shared form of collective intelligence. How, in the future, can we involve civil society in the official discussion about quality?'

Good housing, beyond urban development on autopilot

'Good housing must be accessible to every target group on the housing ladder. This can only be achieved by breaking open the housing assignment. There is a clear need for a larger supply (more housing units) and a more diverse, flexible and adapted range of housing units (a larger choice of housing types according to adapted construction and management concepts, with consequently more price variation, especially in the lower segments). In addition, consideration should be given to where this additional residential arsenal should emerge. A city architect cannot be naive in this respect: changing the real-estate market will not be possible. But with a targeted approach, we can try to move a few bricks that can strategically influence the ground swell of opinion about the housing market.

Over the past decades, Ghent has already worked to revalue urban ground-level housing. The pilot projects of sogent (Ghent's autonomous urban development company) combined design quality with making urban owner-occupied housing accessible to families. Today, the challenge lies elsewhere: an affordable rental market. One in two inhabitants of Ghent rents a housing unit, often of substandard quality. The city architect and urban development company are now teaming up to advocate another form of urban development. What if we retain public control of the land and link the granting of business rights on that land to spatial quality requirements? Just build better and affordable housing on urban land instead of selling it. Collaboration with social-housing companies is a matter of course, but collective partnerships (such as housing cooperatives) or private partnerships also offer opportunities.

Generating an impact on the property market also implies re-establishing a dialogue with these stakeholders. Today we are investigating how we can set up a structural and correct way of collaborating with "Gentbouwers", the

Peter Vanden Abeele was appointed as the first City Architect of Ghent in 2017. He has been a guest professor at Ghent University since 2019. He worked as a researcher at Ghent University and as a project manager at AG Vespa in Antwerp. From 2009 to 2011 he acted as urban planning adviser to the City Architect of Antwerp. As a partner of Maat-ontwerpers, he was subsequently involved in the designs of regional projects and complex urban design assignments. As an expert, he is a member of various advisory bodies such as GECORO (Municipal commission for spatial planning) in Ghent and the 'Stadsatelier' (Urban workshop) in Ostend.

professional private builders who design and develop the bulk of the housing market in our city. It is essential to be able to exert influence further upstream in the monitoring process in order to improve the quality of projects. We engage in a dialogue about the intentions and programme of new developments (via a shared and established project definition) and offer guidance in selecting the most suitable designer.

We must have the courage to reflect further on town houses. Too often we see generic terraced houses pop up in allotment plans. In many visually prominent projects dealt with in the Quality Chamber, we come across a design and development production on autopilot. Where is the attention for the power of design? What makes a good floor plan? What happens on the threshold between residential space and street space? Through the conversations in the chamber, always in the presence of both the client and the designer, we increasingly manage to bring about change in this. I want to use the Quality Chamber as a platform to initiate a more mature discussion and to adjust projects, but also to offer design freedom. Innovative projects in the field of denser connected living or collective living, for example, quickly come up against our generic urban planning rules. The Quality Chamber challenges these frameworks and acts as a breeding ground for innovative forms of housing.'

Stefan Devoldere

'Stadsatelier' as platform, designs for the city

'As Flemish Government Architect, you can weigh heavily on public opinion and on future Flemish policy, but at the urban level, as a quality controller, you are much closer to the realization on the ground. A strong relationship with the city council is crucial in this respect. Your mandate is given weight by the partners you work with and the way in which policymakers consider your role in the process to be self-evident. You provide arguments in a local dynamic that you usually do not control, but with the right backing you can steer the playing field. The arguments are important, but above all the conversation is indispensable.

The 'Stadsatelier' (Urban workshop) in Ostend wants to be actively involved in organizing and keeping this conversation going. In my opinion, quality always exists by grace of a well-considered discussion. We conduct it internally among the members of the Stadsatelier, but also with policymakers, building promoters and other stakeholders. One hears what the other says. Intentions are expressed jointly. Shared ambitions are confirmed. New insights are applied. In this way, the Stadsatelier also becomes a platform for synergy within its own municipal services. It is a place where things can be questioned and where connections are made. Not only the word, but also the design is an important instrument in this. We are not a classic quality chamber. We want to weigh on the process as early as possible in order to create the conditions for a high-quality end result. From the start we renamed ourselves Stadsatelier. This means that we help to think about and design the city. We do this in both the short and long term. We give advice on current projects, but we also create a framework for future developments. We do this both technically and in terms of content. We supervise procedures to realize innovative housing projects on private and public land, and we carry out design research into the future of Ostend. Through the projects we set in

---

Stefan Devoldere was chairman of the Ostend Stadsatelier from mid 2015 till the end of 2020. The dean of the Faculty of Architecture at Hasselt University since September 2018, he is currently the chairman of the Stadsatelier Hasselt (formed in 2021). He is a civil engineer and architect and a spatial planner. From 2004 to 2010 he was editor-in-chief of the Belgian architecture magazine A+. A gifted author, he has curated several architecture exhibitions at BOZAR Brussels and the Whitechapel Gallery in London. Between 2011 and 2015 he was deputy Flemish Government Architect and between 2015 and 2016 acting Flemish Government Architect.

motion a gradual transformation of the residential fabric. In the "Global Strategic Development Plan" we outline the vision that underpins this transformation. It is a reference document that inspires policy and sets the tone for reflection on the city.'

Regional spatial policy as a cultural laboratory

'AR-TUR, the centre for architecture, urbanism and landscape in the Kempen region, is exploiting its position as a cultural player in order to have the greatest possible impact on the quality of the built environment in a rural region. As an unmandated cultural organization, it is not easy to exert real influence on supra-local regulations and systems and on local policy. That is why we employ a broad palette of cultural formats with which we mediate, inspire and innovate. We put spatial challenges on the agenda that are urgent locally, but also relevant regionally. We facilitate an open discussion and strive for a shared *Baukultur* among people and organizations.

The Kempenlab is a free cultural space in which AR-TUR explores various formats and themes that we examined earlier in the "Kempenatlas", a study and accompanying publication that yielded a great deal of knowledge about the region's spatial history and challenges. The focus in the labs is often on specific regional and rural challenges, such as in the Kempenlab "Dorpsarchitectuur en Landschap van kerken" (Village architecture and landscape of churches). Kempenlab has a ripple effect: we connect insights and people from concrete local cases with supra-local reflection and knowledge exchange; we build a community of ambassadors—designers, experts, policymakers, residents, clients, entrepreneurs, project developers, etc.—by systematically enthusing stakeholders.

We show stimulating examples from elsewhere. We spread and deepen knowledge. We establish connections between various subjects, stakeholders and places. We initiate design research and support possible spin-off projects. We link problems with possible solutions and with the political momentum that can create windows of opportunity.

Edith Wouters is an architectural engineer. Since 2007 she has been the artistic director of AR-TUR, the centre for architecture, urbanism and landscape in the Kempen, the sandy region in the north of Belgium. She initiated the 'Kempenatlas', a book and exhibition, which was presented as a project for the region. The Kempenlab was a means of sharing knowledge and building alliances in order to have the greatest possible impact on space. In 2016, after having worked as an architect for 20 years, she set up CAPasitee, a cultural architecture practice where she is, among other things, project coordinator for PARCUM, the museum and expertise centre for religious art and culture. CAPasitee is a continuation of her work as an architect at TEEMA and as project manager at the Flanders Architecture Institute.

In this way, AR-TUR builds a robust learning network that transcends the local level. By setting up such processes unsolicitedly, AR-TUR is gradually acquiring a position as a centre of expertise. Local and supralocal authorities and organizations are now seeking advice from AR-TUR and giving assignments. Among other things, we assist local authorities in the selection of design agencies and are actively involved in thinking about regional quality initiatives. In this way we help to increase the spatial quality in the field and new content is generated for the Kempenlab. In the future we want to continue working together in this way on a regional vital architectural climate.'

Quality control is constantly evolving

'Ever since the "Architecture Memo" was approved in 1996, architectural policy and quality control have been high on the agenda in Antwerp. The first City Architect, René Daniëls, was appointed in 1999. The city projects that took shape in those early years involved, for instance, Het Eilandje, the reappraisal of the station area, and Park Spoor Noord. In 2000 the first building aesthetics committee was established. Since the mandate of Kristiaan Borret (2006–2014), the City Architect has been anchored in the city administration with a supporting team. He worked in particular on the team's horizontal operations and the refining of the competition procedure. As the third City Architect, Christian Rapp has continued to build on the legacy of his predecessors while placing his own accents, such as the city along the ring road and the Left Bank.

It is important to specify that the City Architect is a policy adviser. Working from an independent position, he acts as a bridge between the administration and policy. Therefore, he is neither a policymaker nor a real official. In that sense, he relies on dialogue and an open discussion to give shape to that relationship involving the administration and policy. This must always take place in an atmosphere of trust: being on good terms is more important than falling back on your position.

One of the key tasks of the City Architect is good commissioning. As a team, we accompany the municipal services and subsidiaries in their building projects, but also private clients. The instruments at our disposal are by now tried-and-tested recipes. It is thanks to this set of tools that quality control today is inherent to the different urban processes.

This does not mean that the role of City Architect has become superfluous. Attention is shifting to other themes. Whereas in the beginning the focus was on the development of a professional architecture policy within the municipal

---

Katrien Embrechts is an architect with a strong interest in urban planning and management. From 2001 to 2004 she was project manager in charge of the urban development project 'Het Eilandje' for the then City Architect. She coordinated the drafting of the master plan and various visual quality plans for the area. She subsequently worked for AG Vespa as project manager on various city projects. Since October 2006 she has been the right hand of the City Architect of Antwerp, during the mandate of Kristiaan Borret (2006–2014) and Christian Rapp (2016–today). She sits regularly on juries and committees for the city, private parties, and the Flemish Community.

services, today there is a need for quality control in the context of new procedures such as DB and DBFM. In addition, urban challenges are becoming increasingly complex and developments are growing in scale. The evolution of the building aesthetics committee into the comprehensive quality chamber responds to these new challenges. In the early years there was AG Vespa, Antwerp's municipal real-estate company, a pioneer of the fine-meshed bottom-up architectural policy. Just think of the integrated approach in the red-light district where, besides strategic housing projects, social projects were also launched. With the land and building policy, they practised a form of urban planning acupuncture by constructing trendsetting single-family dwellings in underprivileged neighbourhoods. Today, the company has grown substantially and their tasks and partners are more diverse and more complex. As a result, the work on quality continues to evolve, and processes and instruments constantly need to be rethought.'

Moratorium creates conversation space

'Our planning permission policy has evolved into a strictly legal affair. It is only about rights and duties. But that does not guarantee good architecture and good spatial planning: that requires a broader view, and a conversation that does not shy away from words that cannot be so conclusively defined in legally sound terms. Quality chambers offer an opportunity for that discussion.

That conversation is complementary to the legal test, it does not replace it. It explores the margins left by the legal framework. In our country, those margins are often small, because those legal frameworks are defined very strictly. We are familiar with the improbable combination of dissolute spatial planning and patronizing regulations. This has to change, but quality chambers are not the right place for that. Quality controllers should not give the impression that they are above the law, but make their adjustment within those narrow margins: from a necessary evil to a shared ambition.

The legal planning permission policy imposes and prohibits, while quality control suggests and encourages. Quality does not come about by order, but by incentive. A quality procedure is a moratorium, a delay in which the question is whether there is room for improvement. Building parties that want to move quickly can take this into account by planning these consultations in good time and by making a case for quality themselves. In this way, the existence of a quality chamber raises the level, because building parties know that they not only have to tick boxes, but also have to put their ambitions into words. They have to prepare themselves for the conversation.

That is why quality controllers should pay attention to their language. Because they speak in a different register than the lawyers, they must make an effort to speak intelligibly about intangible values. Help can come from

---

Paul Vermeulen is professor of design at TUDelft, where he heads a programme on Urban Architecture. Since 1989, together with Henk De Smet, he has been a partner in the architectural firm De Smet Vermeulen architecten. An author, he enjoys broad international recognition as a researcher and critic. In 2011 he received the Prize of the Flemish Community for Architecture. He has held several advisory roles, including as chairman of the Advisory Committee on Ostend Architectural Heritage (2007–2017), chairman of the Quality Chamber for Monuments and Architecture in Ghent (2011–2015), and expert in the Flemish Government Architect selection committee (2016 and 2020).

architectural criticism and from education, which has to provide mature and well-trained designers, at home in the registers of architectural culture.

The 'Bouwkundig Erfgoed' (Architectural heritage) advisory committee in Ostend was a great experience, because new and much needed policy not only took shape in legal terms, but also in a repeated quality discussion with a great many parties with building intentions. In the space of a few years, this has led to broad support for that policy, including the difficult dilemmas it sometimes involves. Parties that were initially reluctant took advantage of the delay provided by the discussion to reconsider their attitude and make good decisions. They saw for themselves the leap in quality and became its advocates.

We want sustainable and socially inclusive towns and villages. A quality chamber must take this into account in its judgement. But ideally, the broader policy framework covers such values and anchors them in law. But even then, quality controllers must be able to make the difference and weigh up the design quality between equally sustainable or inclusive alternatives. Beauty, soundness, appropriateness: those who do not acknowledge the appeal of Vitruvian values should refrain from quality control.'

Project Credits

Project Credits

Observation tower
Design Team Baeten Hylebos Architecten
Location Sinaai
Year 2019

Zoersel House
Design Team Arjaan De Feyter Interior Architects
Location Zoersel
Year 2007

Masonry House
Design Team Schenk Hattori Architecture Atelier
Location Essen
Year 2015

Silos—Kanaal
Design Team Stéphane Beel Architects
Location Wijnegem
Year 2016

Studio SDS
Design Team GRAUX & BAEYENS architecten
Location Bachte-Maria-Leerne
Year 2018

Youth Centre 'De Lichting'
Design Team Raamwerk
Location Lichtervelde
Year 2019

Chapel of Our Lady of the Muizenhoek
Design Team PULS architecten
Location Muizen
Year 2017

Montigny live-work units
Design Team META architectuurbureau
Location Antwerp
Year 2013

Werfstraat
Design Team Bovenbouw architectuur
Location Brussels
Year 2020

Zegel
Design Team Hub
Location Antwerp
Year 2017

House VDB
Design Team Collectief Noord Architecten
Location Antwerp
Year 2014

Kioskplaats Police Station
Design Team De Smet Vermeulen architecten
Location Antwerp
Year 2014

Office and apartment Bailleul
Design Team Marie-José Van Hee architecten
Location Ghent
Year 2003–2010

Community Centre De Steen
Design Team ono architectuur
Location Bocholt
Year 2013

BLAF tlG
Design Team BLAF Architecten
Location Ghent
Year 2018

One Room Hotel
Design Team dmvA
Location Antwerp
Year 2015

House L-C
Design Team GRAUX & BAEYENS architecten
Location Anzegem
Year 2017

The Majin House, care home
Design Team Raamwerk and Van Gelder Tilleman Architecten
Location Ghent
Year 2019

VDB social housing
Design Team VERS.A
Location Elsene
Year 2021

Project Credits

Lalo
Design Team murmuur architecten
Location Antwerp
Year 2015

Van Artevelde apartments
Design Team BULK architecten
Location Antwerp
Year 2015

Apostelhuizen Studio
Design Team De Smet Vermeulen architecten
Location Ghent
Year 2005

apart huis arts
Design Team architecten de vylder vinck taillieu
Location Kalken
Year 2011

Youth Centre 'Jeunes'
Design Team AgwA in collaboration with Ferrière Architectes
Location Vorst
Year 2014

Maarschalk Gerardstraat 5
Design Team Eagles of Architecture
Location Antwerp
Year 2019

The Little Prince
Design Team Dhooge & Meganck Architectuur
Location Ghent
Year 2016

House Verbrande Brug
Design Team architecten de vylder vinck taillieu in collaboration with Doorzon interieurarchitecten
Location Undisclosed
Year 2016

RLN, rehabilitation centre
Design Team URA Yves Malysse Kiki Verbeeck
Location Ninove
Year 2015

OFFICE 229: Public Library
Design Team OFFICE Kersten Geers David Van Severen
Location Sint-Martens-Latem

Organ loft for the Contius organ, St Michael's Church
Design Team 360 Architecten
Location Leuven
Year 2019

State Archives Ghent
Design Team Robbrecht en Daem architecten in collaboration with Arch & Teco
Location Ghent
Year 2014

Walled house with winter garden
Design Team STUDIOLO architectuur in collaboration with Koen Matthys
Location Ghent
Year 2015

Olijftakstraat
Design Team FELT architecture & design
Location Antwerp

Dambruggestraat
Design Team Dierendonckblancke architecten
Location Antwerp
Year 2015

Twaalfkameren
Design Team Dierendonckblancke architecten
Location Ghent
Year 2010

Double house Kattenberg
Design Team Architecten Broekx-Schiepers
Location Antwerp
Year 2015

Project Credits

Wolters House
Design Team tim peeters architecten
Location Sint-Amandsberg
Year 2018

Prins Leopold
Design Team ono architectuur
Location Borgerhout
Year 2015

Meir corner building
Design Team DMT architecten
Location Antwerp
Year 2006

Langemark-Poelkapelle town hall extension
Design Team Tom Thys architecten
Location Langemark-Poelkapelle
Year 2019

De Nor
Design Team FVWW architecten in collaboration with Dennis Tyfus
Location Antwerp
Year 2018

Media Building
Design Team Robbrecht en Daem architecten & Dierendonckblancke architecten in collaboration with VK Engineering & Arup
Location Schaarbeek (Brussels)
Year Project 2014–2019

Elementary School Zarren
Design Team FELT architecture & design
Location Kortemark
Year 2018

Schaerdeke social housing
Design Team Architectenbureau Bart Dehaene in collaboration with artist Dirk Zoete
Location Lo-Reninge
Year 2019

DC-V house and office
Design Team Vermeiren—De Coster Architecten
Location Antwerp
Year 2014

Verzoeningstraat
Design Team Poot Architectuur
Location Borgerhout
Year 2010

Broek
Design Team Tim Rogge Architectuur Studio
Location Deurle
Year 2020

Soubry
Design Team Coussée & Goris architecten
Location Moen
Year 2002

Service building container park
Design Team ectv architecten Els Claessens en Tania Vandenbussche
Location Jabbeke
Year 2009

Ryhove Urban Factory
Design Team Trans architectuur stedenbouw
Location Ghent
Year 2018

Main Partners

Main Partners

DELEN
PRIVATE BANK

www.delen.be

Main Partners

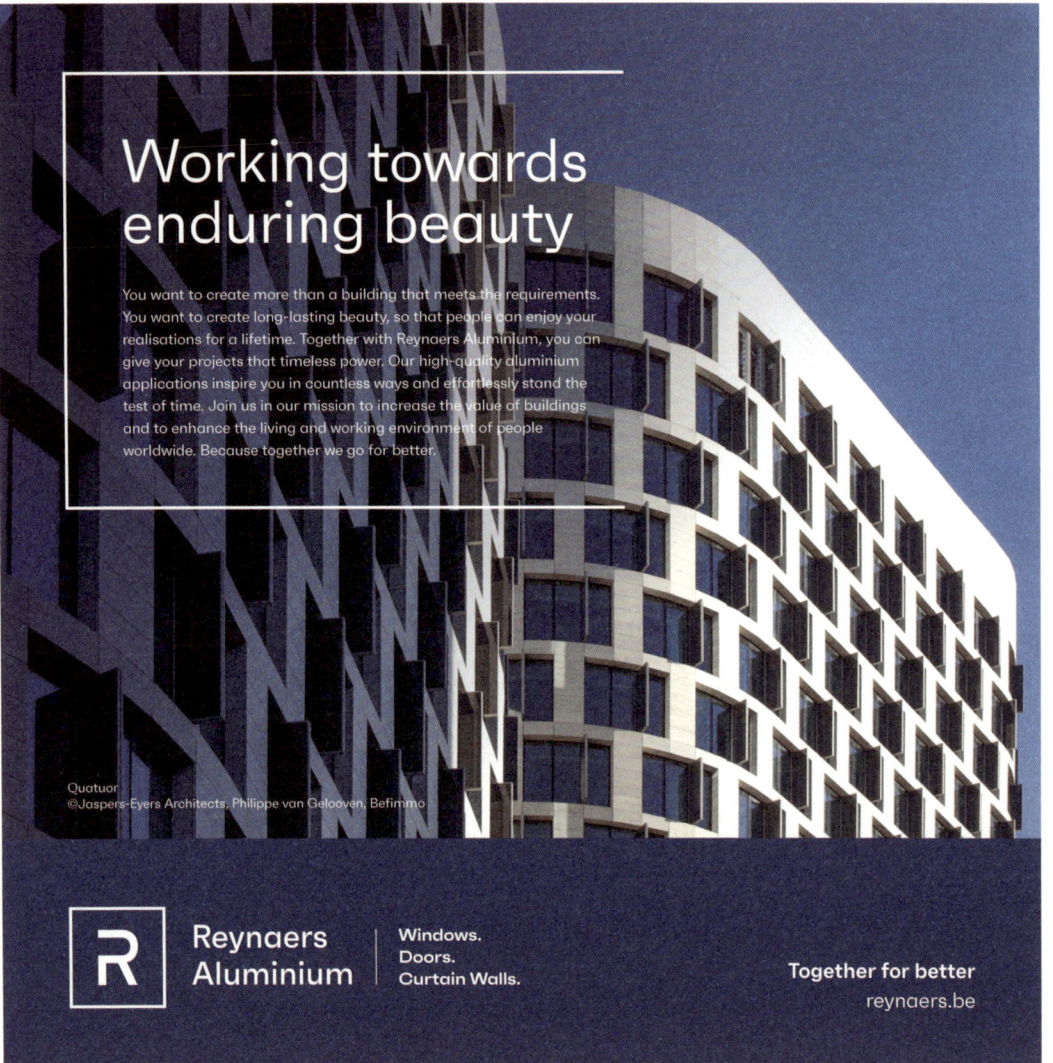

Partners

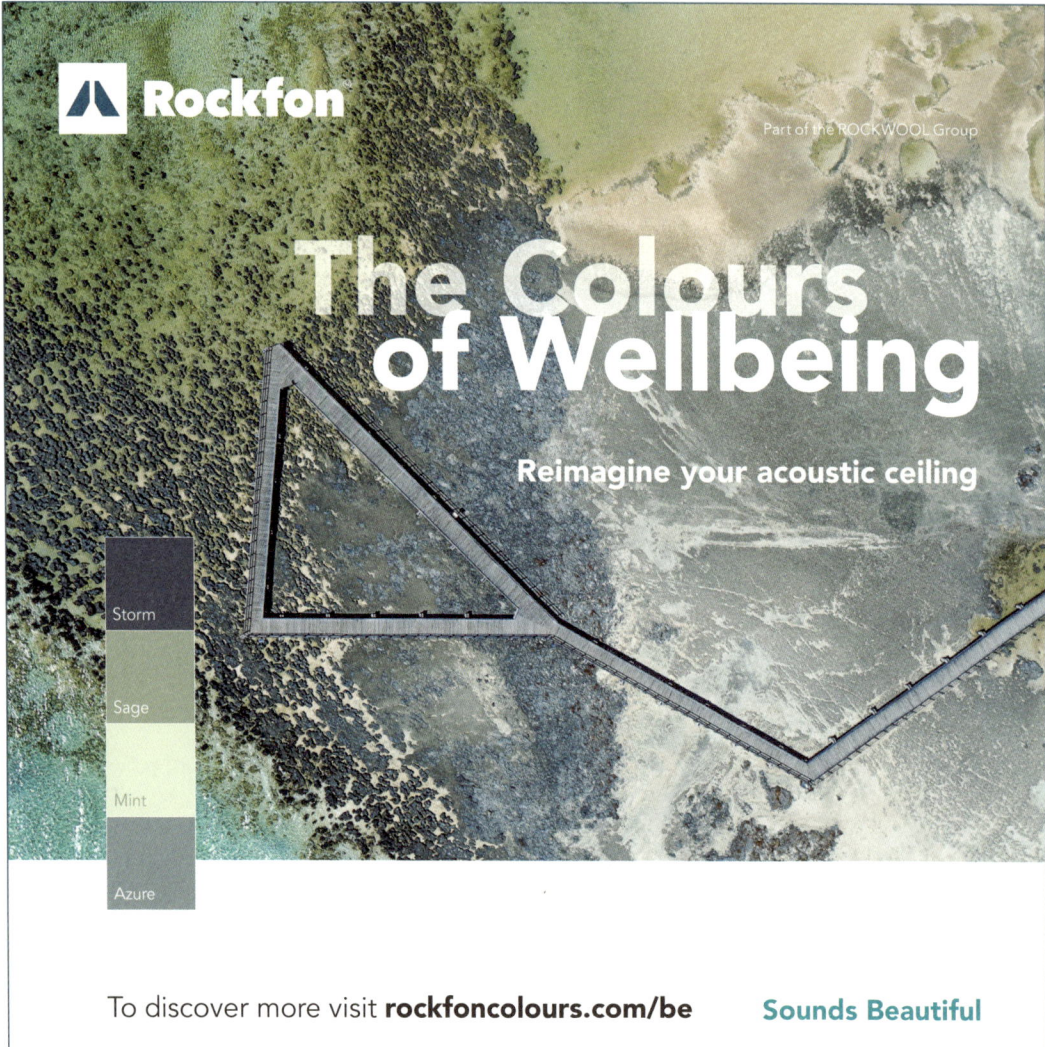

Colophon

Colophon

Bovenbouw Architectuur
Composite Presence

This book was published on the occasion of the *Composite Presence* exhibition in the Belgian pavilion at the 17th International Architecture Exhibition in Venice, Italy. The exhibition was commissioned by the Flanders Architecture Institute and developed by Bovenbouw Architectuur. The exhibition and publication are a production of the Flanders Architecture Institute on behalf of the Flemish Minister for Culture, Jan Jambon.

Editors
    Sofie De Caigny
    Dirk Somers
    Maarten Van Den Driessche
Authors
    Kristiaan Borret
    Irina Davidovici
    Sofie De Caigny
    Louis De Mey
    Stefan Devoldere
    Katrien Embrechts
    André Loeckx
    Christian Rapp
    Leo Van Broeck
    Peter Vanden Abeele
    Maarten Van Den Driessche
    Paul Vermeulen
    Edith Wouters
Published
    © 2021 second edition

Registered publisher
    Sofie De Caigny, Director
    Flanders Architecture Institute
    Jan Van Rijswijcklaan 155
    B–2018 Antwerp, Belgium
    www.vai.be
Flanders Architecture Institute Coordination
    Nino Goyvaerts
Production assistance
    Ilse Degerickx
    Hülya Ertas
    Petrus Kemme
Bovenbouw Architectuur Coordination
    Esmeralda Bierma
    Myrthe Geelen
    Alex Turner
    Eva Wollaert
Graphic Design
    Joris Kritis with Terry Kritis
Photography
    We Document Art
Translation and copy-editing
    Patrick Lennon
Printer
    die Keure, Bruges
Paper
    Munken Pure Rough
Cover Image
    We Document Art
Distributor
    Exhibitions International, Leuven

ISBN 9789492567208
Legal Deposit D2021/10.202/1

All images © We Document Art
Except for
360 architecten [103] / AgwA [91] / Baeten Hylebos Architecten [21, 45] / Luca Beel [63 (right)] / Stijn Bollaert [47, 55, 73, 79, 81, 107, 129, 143] / Bovenbouw Architectuur [12, 61] / Dennis Brebels [115] / Hilde D'haeyere [141] / Michiel De Cleene [14] / Petra Decoutere [83] / Dennis De Smet [133 (left)] / De Smet Vermeulen architecten (photo: Filip Dujardin) [67] / De Smet Vermeulen architecten (photo: Frederick Vercruysse) [87] / Filip Dujardin [59, 71, 89, 95, 97, 99, 105, 111, 113, 119] / Eagles of Architecture [93] / FVWW architecten (photo: Ans Brys) [19, 125] / Bart Gosselin [75] / David Grandorge [69] / David Griffin and Hans Kolhoff [22] / Jan Kempenaers [24] / Jan Liégeois [51] / Maps and Plans, KBR [15] / Yannick Milpas [133 (right)] / André Nullens [121 (left)] / Olmo Peeters [65] / PULS architecten [20, 57] / Daniëlle Raymaekers [63 (left)] / Luc Roymans [135, 137] / Schenk Hattori Architecture Atelier (photo: Matilde Travassos) [49] / Studio Joost Grootens [16] / Team Vlaams Bouwmeester (photo: Filip Dujardin) [23], (photo: Niels Donckers) [17] / Thomas Schütte, Collection Herbert Foundation [18] / Johnny Umans [117] / Dieter Van Caneghem [131] / Wim Van Nueten [121 (right)] / Crispijn van Sas [123] / Vercruysse Dujardin [139] / Jeroen Verrecht [53, 77] / Tom Verstraeten [85]

© 2021
Flanders Architecture Institute

All rights reserved. No part of this publication may be produced, stored in an automated database or published, in any form or by any means, whether electronic, mechanical, by photocopies, recordings or any other manner, without the prior written permission of the publisher. Individual authors are responsible for the contents of their contribution.

The publisher has made every effort to abide by copyright laws, but the origin of some of the reproduced documents has not always been established with certainty. Anyone who believes they can assert their rights is requested to contact the publisher.

Colophon

Commissioner
  Flanders Architecture Institute
  Sofie De Caigny
Curator
  Bovenbouw Architectuur
  Dirk Somers
Scenography
  Bovenbouw Architectuur
  Dirk Somers
  Esmeralda Bierma
  Laurids Bager
  Caroline Boeckx
  Myrthe Geelen
  Amelie Pretsch
  Jakub Srnka
Coordination exhibition
  Flanders Architecture Institute
  Nino Goyvaerts
Exhibition production
  Malgorzata Maria Olchowska
  York Bing Oh
  Jurgen Claesen ᶻᵒᵒᵐⁱⁿ'
  Ingrid Crauwels ⱽᴬᴷ
  Kris Delacourt ⱽᴬᴷ
  Vincent de Roover ⱽᴬᴷ
  Jef Merckx ⱽᴬᴷ
  Kilian Price ⱽᴬᴷ
  Sanne Roels ⱽᴬᴷ
  Renate Vlaeminck ⱽᴬᴷ
  Ivo Claesen ᶻᵒᵒᵐⁱⁿ'
  Yosse Claesen ᶻᵒᵒᵐⁱⁿ'
  Stefaan De Maeyer ᶻᵒᵒᵐⁱⁿ'
  Frank de Wit ᶻᵒᵒᵐⁱⁿ'
  Leonie Mackenbach ᶻᵒᵒᵐⁱⁿ'
  Bas Maris ᶻᵒᵒᵐⁱⁿ'
  Elisabeth-Loura Wals ᶻᵒᵒᵐⁱⁿ'
  Laurids Bager Bovenbouw Architectuur
  Esmeralda Bierma Bovenbouw Architectuur
  Jolien de Nijs Bovenbouw Architectuur
  Myrthe Geelen Bovenbouw Architectuur

  Amelie Pretsch Bovenbouw Architectuur
  Jakub Srnka Bovenbouw Architectuur
  Jules Verhaest Bovenbouw Architectuur
Communication
  Egon Verleye
Jury
  Sofie De Caigny
  Vlad Ionescu
  Leo Van Broeck
  Hera Van Sande
  Nina Serulus
  Mechthild Stuhlmacher
Special thanks to
  Sarah Adriaenssens
  Filippo Arenosto ᴼᶠᶠᴵᶜᴱ
  Agniezka Batkiewicz ᵗⁱᵐ ᵖᵉᵉᵗᵉʳˢ ᵃʳᶜʰⁱᵗᵉᶜᵗᵉⁿ
  Marine Boey
  Edoardo Cimadori
  Geert De Proost
  Sabine De Vylder
  Suriya Guerzoni-Verschuere
  An Jacquemain
  Fred Meeuwens
  Chris Merckx
  Meta Noyens
  Giulio Piovesan
  Hélène Reychler
  Sievi
  Henri Smid ᴿᵃᵃᵐʷᵉʳᵏ
  Quinten Smolders
  Mihran Topbas
  Bart Tritsmans
  Niko Van Horenbeeck
  Stan Van Pelt
  Milo van Snick
  Tuur Vermeiren
  Miriam Vervliet
Team Vlaams Bouwmeester
  Tania Hertveld
  Catherine Robberechts
  Erik Wieërs

Atelier stadsbouwmeester Antwerpen
Katrien Embrechts
Christian Rapp
Valerie Van de Velde

Stadsbouwmeester Gent
Bregje Provo
Peter Vanden Abeele

and all of the participating architects

Commissioned by

With the support of

With the additional support of

Cultural partner

Main partners

Additional partners

Rockfon
Kubus
Vectorworks
Sto
Knauf

STADSBOUWMᵐᵉˢTᵐR
GENT